THE STARS AND THE CHAKRAS

THE STARS AND THE CHAKRAS

The Astrology of Spiritual Unfoldment

JOAN HODGSON

THE WHITE EAGLE PUBLISHING TRUST
NEW LANDS · LISS · HAMPSHIRE · ENGLAND

First published September 1990
Reprinted in paperback with corrections January 1997

© Joan Hodgson, 1990

British Library Cataloguing in Publication Data

Hodgson, Joan
The stars and the chakras : the astrology of spiritual unfoldment.
1. Astrology   2. Chakras
I. Title
133.5
ISBN 0-85487-082-2 (hardback, out of print)
0-85487-100-4 (paperback)

*Set in 11 on 13pt Galliard on Apple Macintosh
Computer at The White Eagle Publishing Trust,
9 St Mary Abbots Place, London W8 6LS, and printed in
Great Britain at the University Press, Cambridge*

CONTENTS

ACKNOWLEDGMENTS

The publishers would like to thank the following, for permission to quote extracts from copyright works in the text of this book. Unwin Hyman Ltd, for the quotations from LIGHT ON YOGA and LIGHT ON PRANAYAMA by B. K. S Iyengar, © George Allen & Unwin (Publishers) Ltd. L. N. Fowler, Ltd, for the extracts from ESOTERIC ASTROLOGY, by Alan Leo. Sangam Books (Orient Longman) for the passage from SURYA NAMASKARS by Apa Pant. A. P. Watt Ltd and the author for the quotations from James Vogh's ARACHNE RISING, © James Vogh.

TABLE OF CHARTS AND DIAGRAMS

INTRODUCTION

THE WORK OF the White Eagle Lodge for more than fifty years has been built on teaching from spirit, principally from the wise being who wishes to be known simply as 'White Eagle'; teachings which were given through my mother, Mrs Grace Cooke. At the very outset of the work, however, a series of messages was received through her mediumship from another soul who identified himself by the earthly name of Arthur Conan Doyle. The date was 1931, the year after Sir Arthur's passing.

These messages were first published with the full story in THY KINGDOM COME, and later in a revised version with the title THE RETURN OF ARTHUR CONAN DOYLE. These books tell the story of the dramatic release of A.C.D.'s unexpectedly imprisoned soul, and were originally intended to help the seeker understand more clearly the experiences awaiting the soul after the death of the physical body.

White Eagle said that Sir Arthur was one of a timeless brotherhood of humanity's servers. This is fair, for he had devoted his latter years to trying to spread the truth of the soul's survival after death, not least in order to comfort the millions of people devastated by the loss of beloved sons, husbands, brothers and friends in World War I. A prominent figure in Spiritualism, Conan Doyle had given all his strength to propaganda work for its cause in many parts of the world; and his last act before his passing was to struggle to London with a deputation to the Home Secretary, to try to bring about the repeal of the old witchcraft laws under which mediums could be prosecuted and imprisoned.

We read in the books how Conan Doyle discovered that conditions after death were nothing like as simple as he had been led to believe; that communication between the two worlds was far more tricky and difficult than he had imagined, and that he himself seemed after death almost to have been entangled in a spider's web which bound him to the conditions of earth and a rather dream-like state of confusion, until he was freed by a powerful beam of light which enveloped and released him, giving him a vision of a tremendous task which he, in company with a group of wise teachers in the East, had undertaken to perform.

This task was to bring to the world not only a clearer knowledge of the after-death state, but of the path of progress towards a wonderful state of enlightenment and joyous fulfilment, open to every soul that consciously sets forth on the path of spiritual unfoldment.

The story of how these messages were given, and the events leading up to them, even now seems quite extraordinary to those of us who were involved in the original work. Nor is it easy to understand why there was not more general acclaim and acceptance of them, except inasmuch as they questioned so many widely-held beliefs. But the messages were to be only the beginning. After THY KINGDOM COME was published, it soon became clear that here was a teaching which must not remain hidden in a book. It must be lived and demonstrated in everyday life. The beautiful, simple teachings about life after death and the way in which every soul can learn to hold communion with those they love in the world of light had to be given in a simple, human, loving way which every man, woman and child could understand. For this purpose, first a small group of co-workers gathered together as a brotherhood to hold regular groups for meditation, in which they were trained by White Eagle to use the power of thought—soul power—to radiate light and healing into the world, a world which was about to pass through the 'years of fire' long predicted by the guides and teachers who were then the leaders of Spiritualism. White Eagle was, of course, one of these teachers.

It was with the help of the Polaire Brotherhood in France, a group which came into being in an extraordinary way, since described in the book THE RETURN OF ARTHUR CONAN DOYLE, that Brother Nobleheart (as White Eagle called Sir Arthur) was freed; and it was also under the power of this group that the small White Eagle brotherhood came into being. The instructions for all the work which followed came through White Eagle from the group of wise teachers in the mountains who—as it were—held the blueprint for the unfolding plan. First the centre in London, the White Eagle Lodge, had to be established, and later—at the right time—a centre in the country where the teachings and philosophy given by Brother Nobleheart, and thereafter constantly expanded and developed by White Eagle, could be put into practice, in services of worship, in training and meditation, in counselling, and— most of all—through healing, both by the laying-on of hands and by what we call absent healing through prayer.

White Eagle wanted the London centre to be called the White Eagle Lodge, a name with a special meaning. A Lodge, to the American Indian, is a place of refreshment; a place where people may come when they are battered and confused by life's problems; where they can come for comfort, for help, and for healing strength.

The White Eagle Lodge came into being on 22nd February 1936, and very soon after White Eagle started training healers to work in a special way through the chakras, the psychic centres of the patient; and also teaching the healers to work with the co-operation of healing angels, who could be drawn to the prayer group through the use of a simple but inspiring ritual. Through the following years up to the present day, this healing has continued until, now, groups all over the world are working according to the method demonstrated by White Eagle and first suggested in the Conan Doyle messages.

Although we as healers started in a simple way, hardly able to believe that anything could be accomplished, we gradually became more and more astonished at the results of this method of healing, which was as effective with souls as with physical bodies. In fact this healing was obviously taking place first at a soul level, bringing to the patient a peace and harmony which before long manifested in improvement at the physical level. Not all patients responded: often it was a question of slow, patient 'keeping on keeping on', to use White Eagle's immortal phrase; but there were enough real 'miracles' to give us increasing faith in White Eagle's teaching about healing. Today, with more than fifty years' experience, we carry on the same work, but (we hope) with deeper understanding. We fully realize that even now we are only just beginning to see the possibilities for a future way of life which can and will transform lives.

During the following years, our understanding of the chakras—the psychic centres—and how they can bring healing and illumination to a soul, has grown. This book is an attempt to describe how White Eagle has helped us not only to open these windows of the soul, bringing an awareness of the inner worlds, but also how—with the help of the planetary angels—we can become attuned to the whole of God's universe, a universe of magic and mystery which is beyond the comprehension of the mortal mind.

We have also realized through the years the wonderful outworking of the original plan which lies behind this work, and of the way in which souls all over the world appear to have incarnated with a mission to help forward this work of the brotherhood of the New Age. We have come to recognize dear souls who come along, occasionally from remote places in the world, drawn sometimes by the most unlikely means to seek the Lodge; and as soon as they enter the building, either in London or at New Lands, they say, 'I feel I have come home....'.

When the Arthur Conan Doyle messages came through, none of the group involved knew very much about astrology; but quite soon after this (quite young at the time) I found a book by Alan Leo, in a friend's bookcase. I borrowed it, and immediately felt fired with enthusiasm to know more about this subject. A little later, on a railway journey, my mother, Grace Cooke, found herself talking to A. G. S. Norris, author of the book TRANSCENDENTAL ASTROLOGY. Knowing my suddenly-awakened interest in this subject, she invited him home. Soon he had taught me to set up a birth-chart and guided me to the best astrology textbooks then available. As this occurred just before my twenty-first birthday, I was then able to acquire a splendid working library of astrology books and was soon writing horoscope delineations for an increasing number of friends. This was before the dedication of the London Lodge, but once it opened I found myself giving lectures and lessons in astrology, work which continues to this day.

This astrological knowledge has been used through the years in the healing work, in a simple way; but as our knowledge of the chakras developed I became increasingly interested in how they were related to the planets—and indeed the planetary angels. We also began to realize how each of the chakras is related to a different plane of consciousness in the inner world, and how—through that chakra—we are building a subtle body, a vehicle through which we can function adequately on that plane. It is a spiritual law that to function in any dimension of consciousness one needs a body suited to that dimension. On the physical plane we need a physical body, which is the outer coat only of the soul body: which, in turn, consists of a number of subtler bodies to enable it to function on any plane of consciousness. Both White Eagle and Sir Arthur Conan Doyle refer to these planes of consciousness and there is a convenient table illustrating them in THE RETURN OF ARTHUR CONAN DOYLE. When we come to think of the various bodies of man, we may realize that the planes are not consecutive but interpenetrate each other just as the bodies do: the physical body and the lower etheric, closely associated with it; the higher etheric, the astral, the lower mental body; and, associated with the higher centres, the higher mental body and the celestial or causal body, leading the individual all the way through to cosmic consciousness. These different vehicles, or bodies, are related to and affected by the seven traditional planets, from Saturn (the lowest), through Jupiter, Mars, Venus and Mercury to the Sun and Moon.

In this book I am trying to clarify what practical experience is teaching us concerning man's relationship to the whole universe, the planets and the Cosmos. We are all cells in the great body of the Cosmos, and yet every soul is a universe in miniature. Gradually this universe is being created through many, many incarnations, during which we are slowly building and strengthening the different vehicles of consciousness which will link us not only with the Sun, but with all the planets. We believe that there will eventually be no need for space-ships to visit outer space, for within every soul there is an instrument to be developed which can bring us into conscious communication with the planetary beings.

Through the years the White Eagle work has developed into what is becoming a world-wide brotherhood of the spirit. It is with delight and astonishment that White Eagle workers in any of the Lodges and Groups all over the world, when visiting another Group, so often feel a sense of home-coming, a sense of being enfolded by the same white wings of love and protection as have enveloped this work from the very beginning. As Conan Doyle said in one of his earlier messages, long before any of us had any idea of the work ahead: 'There are mightier powers behind this work than the guides and spirit friends usually encountered in our intercourse with the beyond, bringing us to a realization that this work might some day come to be regarded as a forerunner of a new epoch in religion, philosophy and medicine'. An editorial note by Ivan Cooke: 'A fantastic statement...we are content to let time decide'.

1

THE HARMONY OF THE SPHERES

Look how the floor of heaven
Is thick inlaid with patens of bright gold;
There's not the smallest orb which thou behold'st
But in his motion like an angel sings,
Still quiring to the young-eyed cherubins:
Such harmony is in immortal souls;
But while this muddy vesture of decay,
Doth grossly close it in, we cannot hear it.

                                        Shakespeare

THROUGHOUT THE ages, man has looked at the starry heavens with wonder and awe. Great poets, musicians, artists and mystics have sensed in the movements of the stars and planets those harmonies which are in immortal souls, and have endeavoured in their lives and work to convey something of the beauty of those heavenly spheres of consciousness to those of us still grossly closed in 'this muddy vesture of decay'.

The heavenly bodies are also the source of some of our deeper symbols. All over the world, and throughout time, the Sun has been worshipped as the source of life and light. Our lives are ordered by his rising and setting, and by the rhythm of his seasons; and deep within every soul is an instinctual recognition that behind the physical Sun there shines an eternal and immortal spirit, the creator of all things.

17

In every religion, the Sun represents the king, the leader: the saviour through whom the glory of the light shines to heal, to strengthen, to bless and uplift his people. He demonstrates a way of life which will help them become responsive to the celestial harmonies, for those harmonies indeed *are* in immortal souls. Quiet meditation upon the ancient symbol of the Sun, the dot at the centre of a circle, can lead the soul to an increasing realization of the immortality of the human spirit clothed in mortal flesh.

At night the same symbol is apparent as we watch the constellations move in an everlasting circle round the Pole Star. Again this signifies the eternal spirit, the light in the human heart, which guides every soul on its path of earthly experience.

The changing phases of the Moon, reflecting the Sun's light from different angles as she circles the earth, are also a continual reminder of this eternal circling (or spiralling) motion which is the law of the heavens.

As the Sun is the symbol of the eternal and immortal spirit shining in human form, so the Moon, queen of the tides and centre of the watery triplicity of the zodiac, symbolizes the soul of humanity. She is the Mother, the builder of all the changing forms through which the spirit manifests, ruling the birth, the growth to maturity, and then the decay, death and dissolution of all natural life. Yet in the soul world she works with steady and unchanging rhythm, garnering from the experience of each physical incarnation the materials for building that eternal Soul Temple—the solar body—through which the spirit will perfectly shine. Her symbol, the half-circle, shows the unfinished state of that Soul Temple.

The teacher Pythagoras, from his study of the heavens, regarded God as the Grand Architect, the Grand Geom-etrician, or the Grand Musician of the universe. The infinitesimal dot at the centre of the great circle is the

Source—the immortal and unnameable Source, the creative Word—from which life radiates into ever-increasing circles of eternal love and wisdom, manifesting in the myriad life-forms on earth. The enfolding protecting circle around this creative Word or Sound may be likened to the divine Mother, proceeding from the heart of the Father, and giving shape to the white ether, which in its different degrees of vibration is the basis of all life-forms.

It is as we read in St John's Gospel (1:1-5):

In the beginning was the Word, and the Word was with God, and the Word was God. The same was in the beginning with God. All things were made by him; and without him was not anything made that was made. In him was life; and the life was the light of men. And the light shineth in darkness; and the darkness comprehended it not.

And (1:14):

And the Word was made flesh, and dwelt among us (and we beheld his glory, the glory as of the only begotten of the Father,) full of grace and truth.

The Word is God, and the Word dwells in the flesh—in the heart of every soul. Although it is enveloped in layer upon layer of etheric matter of different degrees of density, eventually we *shall* behold his glory in every human soul, as the glory 'of the only begotten of the Father, full of grace and truth'. This was perfectly demonstrated for mankind in the life of Jesus of Nazareth, who showed the Way of every soul towards the building of the glorious solar body, the temple of the living God. It has been demonstrated in the lives of saints and seers, masters and adepts throughout the ages, but according to White Eagle the most perfect manifestation was shown through the life and works of the Master Jesus.

In the creation of the Soul Temple, the Moon, the divine Mother, calls into action the seven great planetary angels—the angels round the throne of the Sun—to assist in the building not only of the physical body, which is the outermost vesture of the etheric bodies—'this muddy vesture of decay'—but also all the subtler bodies through which the manifold gifts of the spirit will be able to manifest. These subtler bodies are built from varying grades of etheric matter. Thus the lower etheric body, which permeates the physical, is mortal like the physical; but the higher etheric lives on and becomes the immortal body of light in which the lower and higher astral bodies, the lower and higher mental bodies, and finally the celestial body, gradually develop and grow until the soul becomes—as described in St John's Revelation—the woman clothed with the Sun, the bride of Christ.

These subtler bodies are closely linked with centres of psychic energy known as chakras which in the physical body are associated with important nerve centres, and with the ductless glands. The principal chakras are:

1. The root-support or *muladhara* chakra, situated at the base of the spine, just above the anus.

2. The sacral or *svadhisthana* chakra, situated above the generative organs.

3. The solar plexus (Sun centre) situated just above the navel, and formed of the *surya* and *manipuraka* chakras.

4. The heart, or *anahata* chakra, situated over the physical heart, but more in the centre of the breast.

5. The throat or *visuddha* chakra, situated in the hollow of the throat at the base of the neck.

6. The brow or *ajna* chakra, situated between the eyebrows.

7. The crown or *sahasrara* chakra, situated in the centre of the brain.

In the book of Genesis we are told that God created heaven and earth in seven days. The significance of the number seven comes to us from antiquity, and it indicates a cycle of development which can apply equally to the individual soul, the soul of a nation or the soul of the world.

It is interesting that our seven-day week is linked with the four phases of the Moon as she travels round the earth, just as the months of the year are linked with the passage of the Sun through the signs of the zodiac. The days of the week have been named after the planets (including the Sun and the Moon) which govern each new day as it dawns. (See my earlier book, PLANETARY HARMONIES, pp. 32-35.)

Because the lunar cycle brings us, in a seven-day cycle, the vibrations of each planet in turn, we are reminded of the powerful effect of the Moon in our everyday lives, the experiences of which are gradually building the Soul Temple, the immortal solar body. The Moon's position in the birth-chart shows the personality of the present life— that part of us which can be easily recognized by our companions. It also indicates our instinctive emotional response to everyday happenings, a response which gradually builds our future.

From ancient times, before the discovery of the extra-Saturnian planets Uranus, Neptune and Pluto, astrologers and alchemists have listed the planets in order of their rapidity of motion as seen from the earth. Starting either with Saturn as the slowest, or the Moon as the fastest, we see that the Sun is always at the centre:

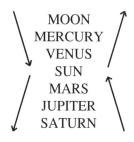

TABLE I: THE ANCIENT ORDER OF THE PLANETS

21

Setting out the planets in this way, we may see the Sun depicted as the child of God: the golden child, shining deep in the heart of every soul incarnate in the physical world. The Sun, central and eternal source of life and light, is given the symbol of the dot within the circle, the point of light and life within the circle of divine love, the infant sun within the human heart. This point of light is also one with the Sun at the heart of the universe, the Sun which controls and illumines all the planets. The Sun is the divine fire at the heart of our being which will eventually direct and illumine the physical body and all the subtler vehicles linked with the planetary angels, so that we shall indeed hear the harmonies of the spheres which sing in our immortal souls.

In THE LIVING WORD OF ST JOHN White Eagle gives a most helpful description of the mystery of the ensoulment of the Word—the spirit:

'Confusion still exists concerning the nature and functions of the soul and also of the spirit of man. Once spirit comes down to dwell in the flesh it starts to create what is called a soul, for soul is that part of man's being which is built up through experiences undergone by the tender inner self of man during incarnation. Soul can further be described as the feminine aspect of man's life, the mother principle. The soul of the world is made up of the feeling of the world, the soul of a nation is created by the feeling of the people of that nation.

'In esoteric teaching you will always find the soul referred to as representing the mother or feminine aspect of life, the second principle—the first principle being divine will, the father or masculine aspect. In Genesis the story is told how the woman is taken from the region of the heart of the first man, Adam: while Adam lay quiescent God brought forth from his "rib", or heart, the woman— the second principle.

'We should learn to recognize the importance of this soul, this woman aspect; lacking a soul, the first principle in man could not continue to evolve. Adam needed that second aspect to complete him. He had to become ensouled to enable him to live fully. Soul gives feeling to the self of man and it is the intuitive part of man. (The coming Age of Aquarius will bring the mother or woman aspect of life into greater prominence. In other words it will usher in greater development of intuition and an increase of soul power among the peoples of the earth.)'

In the next chapter we shall describe the soul of man in greater detail.

2

THE SOUL AND THE
ASTROLOGICAL ELEMENTS

JUST AS THE sun clothes itself with its planetary system, so
the spiritual Sun in mankind clothes itself with vehicles of
consciousness each on its own etheric wavelength according to the plane on which it manifests. For it is an occult
law that to function adequately on any plane of being, a
soul must have a body vibrating in harmony with the
etheric substance of that plane. As the babe in the physical
womb gradually builds and perfects the different organs of
the physical body, so the soul gradually builds those subtler
bodies which will eventually enable it to function on every
sphere of consciousness, thus fulfilling the divine plan
which is that of the man–woman made perfect, fully aware
and thus truly the image of God.

The growth of the soul may be likened to the growth of
a baby in the womb of the mother. Every soul is nurtured
through all its stages of development: encased in what
some occult teachings describe as the 'cosmic egg' within
the womb of the divine Mother—who constantly nour-
ishes, protects and upholds her child. That there is this
wonderful protection, this guarding, guiding and nour-
ishing of the solar body within the womb of the divine
Mother, is a thought to dwell on, a mystery which we can
only begin to comprehend in the heart, as we meditate on
the divine-Mother aspect of God, symbolized in astrology
by the Moon. No soul is ever left outside the divine love

and care, outside the perfect Plan for the development of the soul body.

The Moon, mother and creator of all form, is placed at the head of the planets in order of their apparent rapidity of motion. This ancient order was regarded as important in mediaeval times, especially in connection with magical practice. When it is time for the spirit—the golden Sun-child—to put down another root into the earth, a ray of light from the eternal spirit, the Sun Self—shines down into the heart centre through the planes of Mercury and Venus, which are the planets between the earth and the Sun in this order, and linked with higher mental and celestial spheres. Here the Sun ray, the divine fire, unites with and quickens the waiting soul to bring about the physical conception, and then descends through the planes of desire, the astral and lower mental and the lower etheric, to be buried as a seed, within the earth, the physical life. The planetary order on the outer side of the earth is Mars (the astral body), Jupiter (the etheric bodies, both higher and lower—immortal and mortal), and Saturn (the earth or physical plane); so that the golden seed, at the time of conception, is buried deep in the earth, represented by the planet Saturn and the root chakra.

The Ancient Wisdom teaches that every organ, every cell of the human body, is subtly linked with the stars and planets in the heavens; and that every soul comes into incarnation under the guidance and direction of the great planetary angels who are agents of the Lords of Karma. These planetary beings are the builders who fashion each organ of the body, under the guidance of the divine Mother, according to the karmic lessons chosen for the coming incarnation.

Moreover, according to eastern tradition, every month of the physical gestation period comes under the influence of a different planet, starting with the slowest, Saturn, and proceeding with the other planets according to the natural order previously described; that is to say, Saturn, Jupiter, Mars, the Sun, Venus, Mercury, and the Moon. The extra-Saturnian planets Uranus, Neptune and Pluto, are omitted from this septenary order as they are not concerned with the child's physical development, but (according to White Eagle and many of the spiritual teachers who have spoken since their discovery in the last two centuries) represent a higher octave of the same planetary rays. By the seventh month the little body is fully formed but not yet ready for independent life, and we start again with Saturn ruling the eighth month, Jupiter the ninth, and Mars—the energetic, individualizing planet—ruling the birth, which seems appropriate to the baby's struggle to make its way into independent life; appropriate also since Mars, through its fire sign Aries, is the essential ruler of the Ascendant and first house of the horoscope, which shows the type of body and general outlook on life.

As the child in the physical womb develops in stages according to the planets in their natural order, so, according to what White Eagle calls the Law of Correspondences ('as above, so below, as in heaven so on earth') it seems logical that the Christ child—that golden seed of the Sun, deep in the heart—will develop the different vehicles of consciousness—i.e. the lower and higher etheric, astral, mental and finally the celestial bodies, according to that same order.

The Sun and Moon represent the positive and negative lifestreams which flow through all creation. The perfect balance between the two creates light and harmony—their imbalance leads to darkness and chaos, both in individuals and nations. The elements connected with signs of the zodiac are in turn positive and negative, the positive being fire and air and the negative earth and water. Each planet manifests its influence through a positive and negative sign; the Sun and Moon, which rule Leo and Cancer respectively, being regarded as the positive and negative sides of the same principle.

The experienced astrologer will be familiar with much of the information in the rest of this chapter, which is an introduction for the general reader to some of the basic ideas to be used elsewhere in the book. Most people are familiar with the twelve signs of the zodiac through which the Sun appears to travel on its annual path round the heavens. This path is known as the Ecliptic, which is divided into twelve sections, each measuring thirty degrees. This circle of equal signs, starting with the Spring Equinox at Aries 0° is known as the Tropical zodiac, and the varying positions of the Sun, Moon and planets as they pass through the signs form the basis of horoscope delineation for the majority of astrologers in the western world.

Some, however, prefer to use a chart of the Sidereal zodiac, which is based not on twelve *equal* divisions of the Ecliptic, but on the positions of fixed stars and constellations which give their names to the Tropical signs. The twelve signs of the Sidereal zodiac are of unequal length, according to the spacing of the constellations near to the Ecliptic.

The two zodiacs require a rather different type of interpretation, but each has its devotees. Zodiac (Greek *zodiacus*) means a circle of animals, and the majority of the signs have animal symbols, as is the case with other zodiacs in many different parts of the world, wherever the stars have been studied. This could well be connected with the Ancient Wisdom teachings, all of which are concerned with the unfolding consciousness of the soul of mankind from the animal to the human, and from the human to the divine.

In practice we have found, over many years, that horo-

27

scopes based on the Tropical zodiac (equal signs) can give an accurate picture of people's character and general outlook on life. They clearly indicate also the type of experiences likely to be met in connection with family, social position, career, finance, health, marriage and other relationships, children, travel, hobbies, etc.

In both Tropical and Sidereal zodiacs the twelve signs are categorized under the four elements fire, earth, air and water, each with three different modes of manifestation, known as cardinal, fixed and mutable. The cardinal signs show the active, energetic, outgoing phase of the element; the fixed signs show its steady, stabilizing and more permanent phase, while the mutable signs give flexibility and adaptability, with a desire for change and variety, preparing as it were for the next experiences of the following element.

In THE PATH OF THE SOUL White Eagle says that the key to the soul lesson for our present incarnation lies in the element of the sign in which the Sun is placed at birth. This indicates the unique soul quality which each individual brings into incarnation, and understanding of this will help in our struggles to overcome egotism and self-will—the chief cause of our human sorrows and mistakes.

The Earth element, linked with the root chakra, firmly grounds the soul in the physical side of life, and its practical issues. The soul lesson of this element is SERVICE, often of a practical and down to earth type; service which helps the more impractical visionary people to earth their ideas and schemes. Those blest with vision and imagination so often have no thought for practical detail, or the time it takes to keep things working smoothly on the physical plane. Being tied to practical issues, as those learning the lesson of the earth element are, can, on the other hand, give a prosaic turn of mind which makes aspiration and meditation difficult and unreal, but will give such souls the patience, courage and tenacity needed in their search for truth. They will find that ritual and ceremonial, precisely performed, together with harmonious sound and colour, will help them to rise in spirit out of the heaviness of earth. They should never think themselves less 'spiritual' than their more visionary brethren, but should try to realize how patient, practical service, kindly and lovingly given, can lift the soul close to heaven, even while it is performing the most mundane tasks.

The Water element, associated with the sacral or spleen chakra, brings the lesson of *DIVINE PEACE*—not an easy path for souls with the water element emphasized, for they are so intensely sensitive and receptive. As we proceed on the spiritual path our energies become increasingly focused in the heart centre, so that we become more vulnerable and sensitive in the feeling side of the nature. Souls learning this lesson greatly need the peace of their own quiet sanctuary, to which they can withdraw for refreshment and protection. They need that strength and inner security which comes from regular periods of quiet withdrawal in meditation, into a chapel, or sheltered garden, or beside still water. They have the ability to draw consciously upon the great ocean of divine strength and peace; but this must be developed by perseverance, discipline and dedication. When they have learned to still the churning waters of disturbed feelings, and through quiet breathing to find the lake of peace within, they will truly realize what White Eagle says in the book MEDITATION: 'as the still water reflects the sky, so the calm soul reflects the image of Christ'.

The Fire element, associated with the *manipuraka* and *surya* chakras (solar plexus) teaches the lesson of LOVE, giving to the soul vitality, energy, vision and enthusiasm, and also a powerful desire nature. Those who are learning the lesson of this element are warm, loving, open-hearted and full of optimism, but although basically kind-hearted, they are often thoughtlessly unaware of the sensitivity and susceptibility of their companions, whom they hurt by tactless speech and action. The lesson of love, so deep and far-reaching, has to be learned on every plane of being. A tremendous range of fiery feelings must be experienced until, gradually, the selfish desires and passions, the ambitions and pride in achievement burn themselves out, leaving only a longing for union with God, the Infinite, the Beloved. Then the fiery energies will be expressed in a sublimely healing, sacrificial love, which illumines the whole being and brings light, comfort and strength to many souls.

The Air element, associated with the heart chakra, brings the lesson of BROTHERHOOD through communication and understanding of the needs of others. People with this element emphasized feel the desire to develop their minds through study of science or art, or in some form of communication through the written word or the media. During the new age of Aquarius, there must come not only increasing stimulation of the outer mind, but a balance of that deep wisdom and understanding unfolding through the mind in the heart. The link of the heart chakra with Venus, ruler of Libra, stresses the importance of the balance between the head and the heart-mind. Even now, humanity as a whole, through education and through the media, is being stirred into a realization of the needs of others on a world-wide scale. This is bringing about a stimulation of the heart centre, the centre of feeling and understanding which brings us into close touch with other souls at an ever-deepening level. This surely is the beginning of the brotherhood of the new age.

Although the quickening pace of mental activity and rapid communication causes much strain and confusion, it is also forcing an increasing number of people to seek an inner path of light and peace through meditation, which means withdrawing into the heart centre to search for that line of light and inspiration from the pole star of their own being—the Christ Star within. It is part of the spiritual awakening that comes at the start of the Aquarian Age.

In the Tropical and Sidereal zodiacs the twelve signs are categorized in the same way under the four elements, each with their three modes of manifestation, cardinal, fixed and mutable (see table below).

	SIGN	ELEMENT	MODE
♈	Aries	Fire	Cardinal
♉	Taurus	Earth	Fixed
♊	Gemini	Air	Mutable
♋	Cancer	Water	Cardinal
♌	Leo	Fire	Fixed
♍	Virgo	Earth	Mutable
♎	Libra	Air	Cardinal
♏	Scorpio	Water	Fixed
♐	Sagittarius	Fire	Mutable
♑	Capricorn	Earth	Cardinal
♒	Aquarius	Air	Fixed
♓	Pisces	Water	Mutable

TABLE II: THE TWELVE SIGNS OF
THE SOLAR ZODIAC

When they are placed round the circle of the horoscope, which in its form represents the circle of the heavens round

31

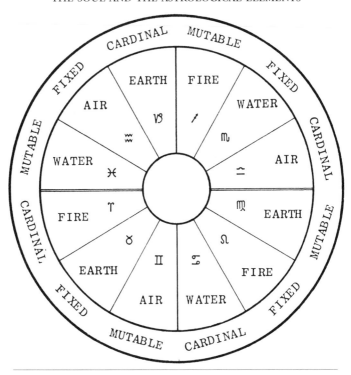

TABLE III: THE TWELVE SIGNS IN CHART FORM

the earth, we may see that the signs of the same quality or mode (i.e. cardinal, fixed or mutable) form a cross within the circle, which is the astronomical symbol of the earth itself.

The planetary rulers of the signs are shown opposite. It is interesting to note that each planet is associated with two of the elements, with the Sun–Moon, Mars and Jupiter ruling fire and water signs, and Mercury, Venus and Saturn ruling earth and air signs. Also, the signs can be seen to follow in order, starting with Leo, top left, down to Capricorn, then round to Aquarius (the latter two both ruled by Saturn) and up to Cancer. This order is something to which we shall return when we consider the planetary vibrations of the chakras.

♌	Leo	SUN—MOON	Cancer	♋
♍	Virgo	MERCURY	Gemini	♊
♎	Libra	VENUS	Taurus	♉
♏	Scorpio	MARS	Aries	♈
♐	Sagittarius	JUPITER	Pisces	♓
♑	Capricorn	SATURN	Aquarius	♒

TABLE IV: PLANETARY RULERS OF THE SIGNS

3

THE PLANETARY BUILDERS

WHEN PLACED in one of its own signs a planet is able to manifest its essential qualities with power and clarity, and is said to be *dignified*. For each planet there is also another sign through which its finest qualities can be expressed. This is known as the sign of its *exaltation*.

When placed in a sign which is the polar opposite of the one in which it is dignified or exalted, it is said to be in its *detriment* or *fall*. When in its detriment or fall a planet's natural power is to some extent inhibited.

It is helpful and inspiring constantly to remind ourselves that all the planetary bodies are but the physical vehicles of the great creative lifestreams which, under the direction of the divine Mother, work together to build different life-forms.* Every soul is indeed a universe in miniature, with vast unrealized potential. The picture that has come down to us of the soul after death sitting on a cloud playing a harp is but a crude representation of how the planetary angels each sound their own note in the universal harmony, and will eventually enable every immortal soul to sound truly the planetary harmonies of their own being, which will be unique and yet part of the grand orchestra of the heavens. This will come as the higher bodies gradually develop through the experience of many incarnations.

*For a discussion of the seven great planetary rays, see White Eagle's SPIRITUAL UNFOLDMENT 2 (especially pp. 45-58), or my earlier book ASTROLOGY THE SACRED SCIENCE.

In the zodiac Saturn rules Capricorn and Aquarius, the signs which are opposite to Leo and Cancer, ruled by the Sun and Moon. Much can be learnt by meditating on the relationship of these three, Saturn, the Sun and the Moon. In Greek and Roman mythology, Saturn was the one-time

	Dignity	Detriment	Exaltation	Fall
Moon	Cancer	Capricorn	Taurus	Scorpio
Mercury	Gemini Virgo	Sagittarius Pisces	Virgo	Pisces
Venus	Libra Taurus	Aries Scorpio	Pisces	Virgo
Sun	Leo	Aquarius	Aries	Libra
Mars	Aries Scorpio	Libra Taurus	Capricorn	Cancer
Jupiter	Sagittarius Pisces	Gemini Virgo	Cancer	Capricorn
Saturn	Capricorn Aquarius	Cancer Leo	Libra	Aries

TABLE V: PLANETARY STRENGTHS AND WEAKNESSES

king of the other planetary gods, and while he held this position the world experienced a golden age of peace, order and culture.

The Moon (which we shall consider at some length) represents both the eternal Soul which is gradually being built, and also the personality of a single incarnation which, while we are in the physical body, we think of as the soul. To distinguish between the two in this book we will always use a capital for the higher Soul, built from many lives; for the single personality of the present life we will use ordinary type. The angels of Saturn guide, guard and protect the Soul which, through their discipline, testing and training, gradually creates for itself a firm, four-square foundation upon which is to be built the temple of the Sun, the solar body. Through the power of the element earth, these angels of Saturn draw the Soul back again and again into physical incarnation.

One of the ancient symbols of the divine Mother is the Tree of Life, and for students of the inner mysteries of the Soul the story of the two trees, the Tree of Life and the Tree of Knowledge at the centre of the Garden of Eden, has deep significance. The Moon, with her alternating light and dark sides, symbolizes Eve, the newly-created child of God, tempted by the serpent hidden in the Tree of Knowledge of good and evil. Adam and Eve are the Son–Daughter of God, created in his own image and likeness—Adam the son or Sun, the divine will and energy, and Eve the daughter, yearning for the wisdom to use the creative power of her heavenly Father–Mother. This urge to learn through life-experience motivates all healthy children, a demonstration of the Law of Correspondences which prevails both in the macrocosm and microcosm.

Once Eve had bitten the apple and given a bite to Adam, they became aware of separate existence; and the angels of Saturn, the administrators of divine law, thrust them forth from the heavenly garden:

Unto Adam also and to his wife did the Lord God make coats of skins, and clothed them.

And the Lord God said, Behold, the man is become as one of us, to know good and evil: and now, lest he put forth his hand, and take also of the tree of life, and eat, and live forever:

Therefore the Lord God sent him forth from the garden of Eden, to till the ground from whence he was taken.

*So he drove out the man; and he placed at the east of the
garden of Eden Cherubims, and a flaming sword which
turned every way, to keep the way of the tree of life.*

(Genesis 3:21-24)

Thus Adam and Eve were drawn into the earth element
to be clothed with physical bodies (coats of skins) through
which they would find both joy and suffering, pleasure and
pain (it is interesting that Saturn rules the skin, the
outermost limit of the body). Through the procreation of
new physical bodies for their young, and the experience of
parenthood and family life, would come the awakening of
selfless love. Also, the creative instinct within them, as well
as the ordinary physical need for food and shelter, would
urge them to work hard to build from nothing, as it were,
some harmony, beauty and security into their lives.

The dual Soul, symbolized by the circle, was separated
at this point, so we now have the astrological symbol of the
Moon, ☽, the half-circle representing both the immortal
Soul and the individual soul, filled with a deep yet often
hidden longing to find reunion with the Beloved, symbolized in Christianity by the mystical marriage between
Christ and his church—the spirit and the soul. It is only
after this mystical reunion (which students of yogic philosophy will appreciate) that the Soul is able to re-enter the
Garden and partake of the tree of immortal life—wonderful symbolism in a simple story.

There is an interesting legend, which takes the story of
Adam and Eve further, known as the Story of the True
Cross. It was popularized in the middle ages in the *Leg-
enda Aurea* (the Golden Legend) of Jacopo Voragine,
inspired Chaucer, and a free translation was printed in
England by Caxton. It was copied in much mediaeval
literature and art, and was illustrated in a series of beautiful
frescoes by the painter Piero della Francesca, which are still
to be seen in the church of San Francesco at Arezzo in Italy.

37

The legend links the tree of the knowledge of good and evil with the cross of Christ. It starts with the death of Adam, when, after a long life of 930 years (Genesis 5:5), he died, to the sorrow and astonishment of his family. This was the first experience of the death of the body in the whole of history. Seth, the third son of Adam, went to Paradise Terrestrial to pray for mercy, and was given by the Archangel Michael (the angel of the Sun) a branch of the tree from which Adam had eaten. Michael told him that when the branch bore fruit, Adam would be restored and made whole. Seth planted the branch on Adam's grave, where it remained and flourished until the time of Solomon.

Solomon found the tree so magnificent that he had it cut down for his palace, but it would not fit anywhere so he used it as a bridge over the river Siloam. When the Queen of Sheba arrived she immediately recognized its significance and knelt in adoration, telling Solomon that her intuition showed her that on this tree should be nailed a Man 'by whom the realm of the Jews shall be defaced and cease'. For this reason Solomon had the bridge taken and buried deep in the ground.

There is much interesting symbolism here, for Solomon represents the development of the wisdom of the outer mind—yet with all his knowledge he could not make the tree fit in his palace. The Queen of Sheba represents the Soul—Eve—the divine Mother, with intuitive knowledge of the path of the Soul, a path which leads to crucifixion on the tree of knowledge of good and evil—or the attainment of perfect balance between the positive and negative lifestreams from which the light is born.

Then follows the story of the Passion in which the tree is found and used as Christ's cross. The cross then becomes the symbol of Christianity; and in Piero della Francesca's frescoes special emphasis is placed on a vision of the cross given to the Christian emperor Constantine the night before a big battle. The vision caused him to carry with him into battle a small and immaculate white cross. Constantine won a miraculous and almost bloodless victory over the forces of Maxentius.*

After the death of Constantine, the Empress Helena discovered the True Cross, through a Jew named Judas, and proved its authenticity. Judas (no relation of Judas Iscariot) knew of the whereabouts of the True Cross and was imprisoned for six days down a well (*n.b.*, deep in the earth) until he offered to reveal them. At the spot, the earth was shaken and a great sweetness came forth. Judas, in joy, cried out 'In truth Jesu Christ, thou art the Saviour of the World'.

In fact three buried crosses were discovered, and Judas had them laid out in the middle of the city. At about the hour of noon the corpse of a young man was brought for burial, and Judas caused the bier to be placed on each of the crosses in turn. Upon the third cross the young man was restored to life.

In the frescoes painted by Piero there is a particularly moving picture of the Empress Helena being visited by the angel Gabriel and told, not of the birth of the Christ, but of her approaching death—and her welcome back into paradise. This at least is the interpretation put on the fresco by Kenneth Clark in his study of the artist, *Piero della Francesca*. A significant aspect of the Golden Legend seems to be the part played by the woman—the Soul. Starting with Eve, in whom the longing for knowledge was

*This reminds us of White Eagle's advice during the blitzkrieg of the Second World War, which led to the poster of a white cross within the circle shining over the rooftops of the city. Under the cross were the words: 'The forces of darkness halt before the cross of light'. There are many stories of the miraculous effect that concentration on this poster had, protecting people and buildings during the bombing.)

awakened, we have the Queen of Sheba with a deeper understanding or intuition than all the wisdom of Solomon, leading finally to Helena's discovery—through intuition—and her holding Judas in the earth, of the True Cross which restored life to the dead youth. The annunciation by the angel of her death was surely symbolic of the Second Death, which every soul must experience before the final resurrection and return to the Garden to eat of the Tree of Life—symbolizing, of course, the restoration to immortality which St Michael prophesied for Adam.

Another interesting part of the symbolism in the story is the age-old picture of the tree as a symbol of the divine Mother, and also of Saturn as the bridge between the two worlds. The return to physical incarnation through the influence of the angels of Saturn may be likened to the Soul putting down roots as the Tree of Knowledge does, to draw upon the wisdom and formative power of the divine Mother. Saturn gives the roots and the basic structure, the trunk and branches of the tree, just as he rules the bony framework of the physical body, and the skin which is its outermost covering. The astrological symbol for Saturn is the half-circle of the Moon beneath the cross of matter, ♄, clearly showing the imprisonment or weighing down of the soul in physical life.

The angels of Jupiter work closely with those of the Moon in distributing the white ether, the formative substance of creation. They are the builders of all form, from the coarse lower and elemental forms, to the finest, the heavenly and celestial bodies. They provide the appropriate garb for the Soul on every plane of existence. Jupiter rules the water sign of Pisces, symbol of the great universal sea of etheric substance which is shaped and moulded by the power of thought. Jupiter is sometimes described as the higher or greater Moon, and, like her, he has a light and a dark phase—a duality which extends his influence from the depths of the ocean of the subconscious self, where dwell the memories of past lives, past hopes and fears, past thought—habits, failures and triumphs—right up to the heights of heaven and the celestial world. His principle is expansion and growth, and he rules both the preconscious, the subconscious, and also the superconscious mind.

The close link between the Moon and Jupiter is shown by the fact that he is exalted in the Moon's sign of Cancer. In the study of the unfoldment of the subtler bodies, the exaltation and fall signs of the different planets can give the astrologer some important keys to deeper understanding. The exaltation of Jupiter in this lunar sign shows how his angels of growth and expansion, of wisdom and far-reaching justice and compassion, work like the sap flowing up the trunk of the tree, or the bloodstream in the physical body, to bring wisdom and strength to the developing Soul. They represent the flowing of the divine life-force through all the different vehicles of consciousness.

Jupiter is especially concerned with etheric substance, which is shaped and moulded by thought. The basic principle is expansion and growth into freedom, so it is understandable that his fall comes in Saturn's sign of Capricorn (the polar opposite of Cancer)—the sign of discipline, contraction and crystallization. Jupiter, so often pictured with wings either on heels or head, finds them clipped when he is in Capricorn, where so often duty and obedience or some physical limitation curtail his freedom. While the astrological symbol for Saturn shows the soul (the Moon) held firmly under the cross of matter, that of Jupiter, ♃, with the half-circle of the Moon rising above the cross, shows the soul striving to rise up into freedom.

From Jupiter we now turn to the next planet in the sequence given. While Jupiter is the distributor of the Moon's creative white ether, Mars, ruler of Aries, is the agent of the solar energy. This is shown by the exaltation of the Sun in the fiery Aries.

Solar energy—through Mars—brings the necessary vitality, energy, will-power and drive to maintain the physical, etheric and astral bodies. It stimulates the impulsive desire nature and lower mental bodies (Aries rules the head and frontal mind), and while it can be immensely creative it can also cause a ruthlessness in the soul which does not hesitate to achieve its ends and satisfy the desires of the lower nature at the expense of others. As Alan Leo says in ESOTERIC ASTROLOGY:

'The next plane below the mental is that of the personal feelings, governed by the planet Mars. This represents the animal man in the fullness of his strength, a force not to be despised or ignored, but transmuted and wisely used, for Mars represents the consciousness of all the cells of the body, including the brain but excepting the heart. The control of desire is necessary before the animal can be conquered and made a useful servant. It is the cerebellum that is the store-house of all the Kamic* or passional force; and Mars, its planetary representative, furnishes the materials for ideation, while the frontal lobes of the cerebrum are the finishers and polishers of the materials, but not their creators. The affinity between Mars and Venus can now be seen, Mars governing the animal sense, and Venus the soul; so that when both are in harmony through attraction, affinity is the result; but when opposed, antipathy or antagonism exists between them.'

Mars is the fiery desire nature which manifests through the astral body. His symbol, ♂, once shown with a cross in place of the arrow, illustrates the solar force energizing

*Kama, in Hindu philosophy, is the desire urge (not to be confused with Karma): as Alan Leo says elsewhere (in THE ART OF SYNTHESIS), it is 'the Hindu Cupid...pre-eminently the divine desire of creating happiness and love...it is only ages later...that Kama became the power that gratifies desire on the animal plane'.)

matter into action. Through automatic reaction this creates karma, which brings the soul, ☽, under the discipline of Saturn, ♄. Yet the exaltation of Mars in Capricorn, Saturn's sign, shows how the solar fire, the golden seed set in the cold earth, strives to grow. Under Saturn's wise discipline and direction, the soul learns the value of patience, endurance, hard work and self-discipline. It gains the strength and endurance of a great mountain, with its peak among the stars.

Besides ruling Cancer, the Moon has close connection with all the water signs. She has her fall in Scorpio, the negative martian sign of destruction and dissolution of form. Yet Scorpio, being a fixed sign, indicates also the permanence of the soul's life beyond the death of the body. There is no death, only a changing condition of the vehicle of the eternal spirit.

In the natural planetary order, the earth's orbit lies between Venus and Mars. The symbol used for the earth is deeply significant, for we see the circle of the Sun, the circle of divine love, covered by the cross of matter. Through this we can catch a vision of that glorious solar energy—the divine fire of life, buried within the earth. This symbol is also similar to the four-petalled lotus within a circle—the eastern mandala of the root chakra, which is related to the element earth, and in which lies dormant the divine cosmic energy known as *kundalini*. B. K. S. Iyengar says of this (in his book LIGHT ON PRANAYAMA):

'The kundalini (kundala = the coil of a rope; kundalini = a coiled female serpent) is divine cosmic energy. The force or energy is symbolized by a coiled and sleeping serpent lying dormant in the lowest nerve centre at the base of the spinal column, the *muladhara* chakra. This latent energy has to be aroused and made to ascend the main spinal channel, the *susumna*, piercing the chakras right up to the *sahasrara*, the thousand-petalled lotus in the head.

Then the yogi is in union with the Supreme Universal Soul.'

This earth symbol of the cross within the circle, ⊕, has been used by brotherhoods of enlightened souls throughout the ages—souls who have been awakened to the glory of the spiritual Sun, and henceforth are prepared to accept the discipline and the constant soul tests of the path which leads to that union with the divine Self, which brings peace and joy beyond all worldly understanding.

Venus is the ruler of the earthy Taurus and the airy Libra; her symbol is ♀. She is the polar opposite of Mars, and their respective symbols show their close link both with the Sun and the earth. The Sun is exalted in Aries and has its fall in Libra. The circle above the cross for Venus represents the heavenly grace of the spirit, the Sun-child within, rising above the cross of matter—the heavenly grace of mercy and forgiveness which is the Christ love, healing and transforming the difficult karma of undisciplined solar energy.

When the soul comes into incarnation, the ray of light or consciousness from the greater Soul shines deep into the heart. It is that still centre of light and truth, almost like a candle flame, glowing deep within the sanctuary of the heart centre. It is the controller and director of our whole incarnation, the true Sun within the heart.

Mars is the instrument of this solar fire, but Venus, the chief planet of the heart chakra, with her calm beauty creates a sanctuary: let us say an altar, deep within the heart, upon which shines the still flame of the Christ Being, the eternal self, the individuality, the *Atman* of Hindu tradition. It is this flame of the eternal self which gradually and imperceptibly, through many, many lives, becomes strong enough to harness and direct the immense energy from the cosmic Sun in the heavens, so that the earthly personality becomes irradiated and transformed. Then the whole life will be lived in a state of perfect harmony and balance between the inner and the outer world.

The Moon's exaltation in Taurus, the fixed earth sign—the sign of the builder—surely symbolizes that eternal Soul Temple which we are all building, and which through the disciplines and effort of the earth life will gradually become a fit vehicle for the full manifestation of the divine solar energy—a physical vehicle through which the solar body can perfectly shine.

The symbol of Mercury is ☿ , a combination of the cross (indicating physical life and consciousness) beneath the circle (the spirit, the inner Sun) with the half circle of the Moon (the soul) above. The influence of this planet, so close to the Sun, can only be fully realized as the soul touches the celestial plane of cosmic consciousness. As Alan Leo states in ESOTERIC ASTROLOGY:

'Mercury is also a planet whose influence is felt more etherically than physically, for its vibrations are far too fine and subtle to be distinguished by those who are not very refined and sensitive, and it is only by way of the nervous system that its influence can act freely. Its physical effects are, more often than not, experienced through its relation with other planets or their aspects.

'Mercury governs Pure Reason or what is known as Abstract Reason, that which is truly human and entirely free from the animal and coarser side of nature, a state which for many is super-human. It is essentially the planet of rhythm and harmony, and therefore adverse positions or aspects to this planet disturb the reason and the higher and purer thoughts and intuitions in man. Its best expression is through the Airy and Mutable signs, with Virgo as a sub-influence, the most etheric of the signs. Its influence alone and apart from the signs can only be felt by adepts.'

Mercury is associated with the throat centre and the element ether. He is truly the messenger of the gods, and holds the fine line of light, the line of communion and communication from the angels of wisdom in the celestial world, through the various planes of consciousness which are ruled by the other planets, right down to the earth life. He rules speech and voice production, and also hearing. As the soul develops the sensitivity and purity of the mercurial vibration it begins to become aware of the celestial harmonies in which the planetary vibrations in the soul are each sounding their own note, which is also colour and fragrance. Thus the angels of wisdom, through Mercury, gradually awaken the soul to cosmic consciousness.

The extra-Saturnian planets Uranus, ♅ , Neptune, ♆ , and Pluto, ♇, along with Mercury have symbols composed of the cross, circle and the half-circle in different arrangements. Their influence and work will be discussed in a later chapter.

4

THE SOLAR AND LUNAR ZODIACS

THE INNER OR soul world is the province of the Moon. In religions all over the world she symbolizes the divine Mother, Mary, Isis, creator and destroyer of form. Her phases as she circles the earth demonstrate to those who are spiritually aware the truth of reincarnation: a continuous cycle of birth, maturity, death, disintegration and then re-birth in a new body. Constantly she creates, destroys and recreates new vehicles through which the Christ Sun can manifest.

Most religions have an outer orthodox form, with stories, legends and parables suited to the needs of ordinary people, the simple stories giving help and guidance in their lives. These stories cover hidden and inner truths too, which can be found by those seeking deeper understanding of the mysteries of life, death and human experience. These inner mysteries are essentially the same in all religions, and basically involve the ancient teaching written over the entrance to the mystery schools of the past: 'Man, know thyself and thou shalt know God and the universe'. It is this inner, soul life of the lunar self which brings to us an awareness of the subtler energies of the Cosmos.

Most people are familiar with the four elements—Fire, Earth, Air and Water—associated with the twelve signs of the zodiac through which the Sun appears to travel on its annual path round the heavens. Not so many students are aware of another zodiac and pattern, based on the Moon's revolutions round the earth in the course of a year, through which are reflected upon the soul of mankind subtler vibrations of the signs of the zodiac. In the lunar zodiac, however, there have to be thirteen signs, because during the year (the solar cycle) there are always more than twelve and less than thirteen lunations (moon cycles).

The Mayans used two calendar systems: the first, based on the Sun, was for everyday practical matters and marked the seasons. The other, which ran concurrently, was known as the 'secret calendar'. It was based on thirteen-day periods and was used for prophecy and magical practice. Long before the astronomers of the Old World had reached any degree of accuracy in their calculations, the Mayan astrologers had tabulated the position of the Moon, Venus and Mars so exactly that they could pinpoint any particular day within a period of 370,000 years! In an old Mayan hieroglyphic manuscript now known as the Dresden Codex are to be found tables of planetary positions which show their calculations to have been practically as exact as those of our modern astronomers with all their sophisticated equipment.

The Celtic Druids certainly used the lunar zodiac, as the Roman writer Pliny tells us: 'It is by the Moon that they measure their months and years'. The Druidic calendar had thirteen months, each of twenty-eight days. An extra day was added to bring it up to the solar year of 365 days. From this came the Irish and Welsh expression, still used in fables and legal parlance, 'A year and a day'.

In order to make their calendar and to study the movements of the stars, Druid astronomers created observatories (or so many archaeologists believe), many of which still exist in France and the British Isles. Professor Alexander Thom has suggested that at least two hundred of the stone circles to be found in these lands were used as celestial observatories. Many of them were designed for predicting eclipses, following the nineteen-year cycle of the Sun–Moon relationship, and also for sighting certain stars. This is particularly evident at Callanish, a group of large standing stones situated on the Isle of Lewis in the Outer Hebrides. There is a ring of thirteen stones, with a central 'great stone', an avenue, and rows of stones obviously placed with a purpose. The avenue appears to be aligned to the rising of the star Capella. The Druids seem to have shown particular interest in this star, which lies in the constellation Auriga, the charioteer; for among the alignments created in their stone circles, Professor Thom discovered that as well as the Sun's eighteen alignments, and the Moon's forty-two, Capella had fifteen—considerably more than the star next in order, Arcturus, which had only eight.

In his book ARACHNE RISING, James Vogh—who has deeply researched this subject—writes:

'Thirteen is an "unreasonable", difficult number, appropriate to the realm of irrational dreams, subconscious fears and desires. The Zodiac of the Moon contains the twelve signs—though with added significance—and also a thirteenth: the sign of pure psychic force.'

Vogh's thesis is that the true significance is precisely this: its connection with the birth of powerfully psychic persons. He claims that the knowledge of the thirteenth sign, far from being remote and obscure, was widely known in ancient times and deliberately suppressed after the Middle Ages.

The Moon symbolizes not only the mother, the wife, and womankind in general, but also the soul life of humanity, that receptive, feeling side of human nature which absorbs and reflects the conditions of the psychic and astral world. From ancient times the element water (and more especially the oceans) has symbolized this soul life. Just as the tides and all the creatures in the sea are subject to the phases of the Moon, so also she governs, far more than we realize at present, the subtler tides of human consciousness; and also that inner world from which we emerge at birth into physical life and into which we withdraw during sleep and unconsciousness, and at the death of the physical body.

In the lunar zodiac we find not only four elements—fire, earth, air and water—but another much more subtle element, ether, which is particularly manifest through the thirteenth sign. This sign is situated in the part of the zodiac between Taurus and Gemini, and there it combines the qualities of Venus and Mercury, those planets associated with the heart chakra, from which there is a line of pure light reaching to the heavenly spheres, a line of communication which can guide every soul on its path.

In his very interesting researches, James Vogh has discovered that this thirteenth sign has been recognized in mystery schools all over the world and that the goddess linked with it in Greek mythology is known as Ariadne. James Vogh writes:

'The Minoan Greeks called her Ariadne, meaning "most pure". A seafaring people, they recognized her power of drawing up the tides, as if by an invisible thread; they suspected that she also drew at the tide of human affairs.

'Ariadne's thread is one of the great magic instruments of Greek mythology. It was the clue which guided Theseus through the dark windings of the Labyrinth. It has become one of the powerful metaphors of all ages; even the word "clue", which once meant only a ball of thread, now means guidance to a hidden answer.'

Arachne, another Greek goddess, was similarly a worker with thread. She wove most beautiful tapestries, and was proud of her work; so much so that Athene, the goddess of war and of wisdom, challenged her to a competition in which they both wove a tapestry, the result to be judged by the gods. Unfortunately for her, Arachne's tapestry—which appeared to depict the thirteen signs of the lunar zodiac—was judged better than Athene's. The goddess was so angry that she changed Arachne into a spider, condemning her to spin forever. Arachne hanged herself, like a spider hanging on a thread, but was raised by the gods into the heavens and her threads of light weave the tapestry of human karma and the pattern of their lives as they make their journey towards the stars. The threads of the spider's web are those links of the psyche which bind souls together through life after life until all hate is turned to love and all debts paid, so that the balance is restored.

The Moon-goddess of the Druids was known as Arianrhod, the Lady of the Silver Wheel (the Moon) who drives her chariot round the heavens. Her reins, like the thread of Ariadne, are the lines of light which guide the soul on its true path. This picture brings to mind also the story of the Bhagavad Gita, in which Krishna drives the chariot of the warrior Arjuna.

The months of the year are, of course, related to the Moon's cycles, as their name implies. In Islamic countries the beginning of the month is marked by the first sighting of the new crescent moon after sunset. Many other races have followed this system of time measurement.

The difficulty with a lunar zodiac is that it is not suitable for marking the seasons on the calendar. The relationship of the Sun and Moon is on a nineteen-year cycle, during the course of which the seasons would gradually change their places in the calendar. For this reason we use the solar zodiac, with its twelve signs, which gives a steady rhythm for the seasons and also clearly depicts the conscious self of mankind. As previously described, the twelve signs fall into logical sections of elements and qualities; three signs in each element of fire, earth, air and water, and four in each of the different modes of manifestation—the qualities of

51

cardinal, fixed and mutable signs. The outer character and mentality is quite well depicted in the solar zodiac and can be adequately described by astrologers who have the intuition to analyse and interpret the planetary positions. The signs of the lunar zodiac fall into the same elements and qualities, but with an additional thirteenth sign which is of the more subtle element ether, combining, as it were, the essence of the other four elements, forming an etheric bridge between heaven and earth. It brings to its subjects intuition and inner guidance, which is the quality needed by all who are attempting to work at the Soul level of consciousness. The subject of a personal horoscope may well be unconscious of the inner feelings which drive him to action, and the intuitive astrologer can often give special help at a deeper level by comparing and balancing both the solar and the lunar positions of the planets.

The constellation Auriga, the charioteer, lies near the Ecliptic, between Taurus and Gemini (its position is shown in a diagram on page 61); and James Vogh, in his research, has found many indications that this constellation is the one related to the thirteenth sign known as Arachne, the spider. The shape and form of the spider's web could be compared with the silver wheel of the chariot driven by the Druids' Moon-goddess Arianrhod, who seems also to be akin to Ariadne, the spinner of the silken thread.

The symbol of this thirteenth sign, which we will henceforth call Arachne, is the cross within the circle, $\oplus$, a symbol marked on ancient stones all over the world. It is the sign of the inner brotherhoods who, throughout the ages, have been drawn together under the Moon, the divine Mother, queen of all magical practice, to use their thought power, which is magical when properly directed, to heal and lead humanity on its path back to reunion with God. The cross within the circle is also significant as the astronomical symbol of the earth.

To fit thirteen signs into the 360 degrees of the zodiac, they each have to be shortened from thirty degrees to approximately twenty-eight. The extra sign, Arachne, fits into the last five degrees of the earth sign Taurus, in which the Moon is exalted, and the first twenty-three degrees of Gemini, ruled by Mercury. We have seen in the previous chapter the subtle and powerful qualities of the planets Venus, linked with the heart chakra, and Mercury, which can only truly manifest its power to link heaven and earth when the soul is totally attuned to the light, to the Christ Sun. Mercury works through the human mind and nervous system; when this is completely still, and under the control of the inner light, the Christ flame can bring heavenly guidance to lead the soul on its path through the many trials and tests of life.

The Druids, like many ancient races, preserved in their stone circles cosmic secrets which were lost when mankind reached the stage when the external mental faculties, those to do with living the everyday life and acquiring technical skills, needed to be fully developed. The active and trained mind of for instance the student, the businessman, the planner, or the researcher, helps to develop the mental body to its full extent. But concentrated thought and effort on the mental plane can also effectively close the door to the subtle, magical lunar mysteries. The ancient stone temples all over the world, such as the stone circles in Britain, and the pyramids in Egypt and in America, were all created at the time when the priests and wise men were still attuned to the cosmic powers. As the teacher Pythagoras told us, 'God geometrizes'. The controlled divine thought power, flowing through the minds and souls of these ancient builders, helped them to transfer into stone the secrets of the universe; their wisdom taught them how to bring into operation on the earth plane the magical power of the stars, impregnated in the stones of these circles, and waiting to be called into service by those who were attuned in true soul brotherhood: those who were able to draw down into the earth, and up from the earth, the divine fire.

White Eagle has often spoken of those 'ancient spiritual fires', buried in the earth in the heart of Britain: the divine fire of the spiritual Sun, drawn down to the earth, impregnating the stones, and buried deep in the sacred places, to be called again into action at the right time. This drawing-down of a divine fire into the earth and impregnating the stones with the qualities of the different stars gives us also the symbol of the divine fire drawn down into the soul at its birth into a physical body. There it is firmly locked in the base chakra, in the element earth, and guarded by Saturn. This sacred fire, *kundalini*, is, as it were, buried in gran-ite—solidified earth—and awaits the awakening of the soul, at the appointed time, before it can be released to rise up the spine, lighting up, energizing, and beautifying each of the chakras, those planetary energy-centres which will each sound their own note as they join in the most glorious music of the stars.

A beautiful picture suddenly and magically dawned on my consciousness after weeks of mental study and working upon this theme. I was taken in spirit, as memory awak-ened, to a ceremony in one of these stone circles aligned to the star Capella. The ceremony occurred at the winter solstice, when the Moon was full, and there came from many places a great gathering of priests, Druids, adepts and wise teachers. They gathered round the central stone within the stone circle. Grouped behind each of the stones, and outside the circle, were gatherings of men and women drawn to a particular stone by some power—they knew not what. There was absolute silence as the teachers led all the people into silent worship. The light from these teachers radiated in most beautiful colours as the power of their thoughts, and their worship of the Sun, stilled all the busy minds and anxious hearts, until all souls became as one in worship. The glorious star seemed to become much larger, like the star which shone on the shepherds at Bethlehem. Its rays touched every one of the stones, and particularly the central stone which became first a great pillar of light, and then a steady pure white fire. Gradually each of the surrounding stones began to vibrate and glow with radiant colour, each also sounding its own note—a most magical combination of sound and colour. Kneeling, we bowed down to the earth in silent worship, and as simple watchers we became aware of great angelic forms standing over the stones, impregnating them with their special vibrations of divine Will, Wisdom and Love. I realized that these stones were not only placed to predict astronomical data. They were placed in their positions to form, as it were, a grail cup, a centre of light through which the earth people could communicate along special lines of light with the other planets and stars. In such conditions as these there *is* no space. In the white stone at the heart of the temple, aflame with divine fire, every brother was in tune with the whole Cosmos and all knowledge available.

The powers which were released were magical, healing, harmonizing and life-restoring. But we were taught that they could be used also for destruction, and that their misuse in the past had caused the destruction of continents and the fall of civilizations. This is why it was essential that the mysteries of the lunar magic should be hidden and suppressed until human development had advanced beyond the selfish animal–human stage and was reaching towards the human–divine. This stage which we all await should come about as the Age of Aquarius–Leo awakens brotherly love in the human heart so that the divine self begins to emerge.

5

THE MYSTERIOUS SIGN OF ARACHNE

The number of Moon periods in each year is always more than twelve and less than thirteen; some means of understanding and adjusting the Sun and Moon year was clearly needed. There are some numerical problems which, without the help of a computer, can be more easily solved through geometry than through numbers. According to Professor Thom, the builders of the stone observatories continually used the Pythagorean right-angled triangle to help them in their measurements and in aligning the stones for different sightings. He states that the builders of stone circles knew, and used, at least six different Pythagorean triangles. The one at Stanton Drew, near Avebury, used the proportion 5:12:13. Of this James Vogh writes, in ARACHNE RISING:

'This last triangle is of special interest, since it forms the basis of a solar-lunar computer. Like the Pythagoreans, the Druids sought geometric solutions to numerical problems, and the 5:12:13 triangle offers a unique "alignment" solution to the problem of reconciling the Sun and Moon cycles....

'The actual number of lunations per year is less than thirteen (line AC) but more than twelve (line AB). Therefore it must be equal to the length of some line (AX) in between.

'In numbers, the solution is formidable. It amounts to dividing 365.2421954...by 29.530588... But geometrically, there is a simple and direct solution: let BX = 3. Then AX = 12.36935...which is the approximate number of lunations per year.

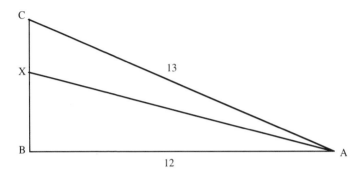

DIAGRAM VI: A SOLAR–LUNAR COMPUTER, BASED ON
THE PYTHAGOREAN TRIANGLE 5 : 12 : 13
The length of the line AX would give the number of lunar
periods in a solar year. (From James Vogh, ARACHNE RISING.)

'Approximate? It registers the number of lunations with perfect accuracy *for any length of time up to a thousand years.*'

The diagram overleaf shows the same 5:12:13 triangle, sub-divided into the twelve solar and thirteen lunar zodiac signs. The short side is sub-divided into five sections which we link with the five elements related to the chakras or psychic centres: Earth, Water, Fire, Air and Ether, and the planets related to these. The experience in life of the action of all these elements gradually helps us to become responsive to the planetary angels. This Pythagorean triangle can lead the astrologer along useful lines of thought, seeing the thirteen signs as reflecting the inner soul life of the individual and the lessons being learned from the birth to the death of the body, and integrated in the inner-world experience into the building of the Soul Temple. When the

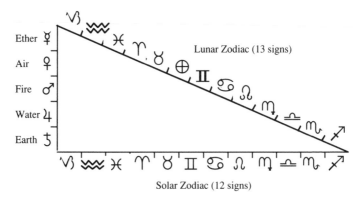

DIAGRAM VIII: THE TWELVE- AND THIRTEEN-SIGN
ZODIACS

time arrives for another incarnation, the line of light from
the Soul to the fresh personality or soul is that silver cord
which is only broken at the death of the body.

In this diagram I have shown each zodiac as beginning
with Capricorn, the sign of the winter solstice or the annual
re-birth of the Sun, and placed the planets and elements in
the order of the chakras, from the base of the spine to the
throat (as we shall describe them in later chapters), to show
how gradually, through experiences of physical life, the
inner Soul life (the lunar zodiac) develops, and the planetary energy-centres, the chakras, are gradually brought
into action, so that the Soul brings into being its own
planetary universe.

The solar zodiac shows the physical consciousness, the
self we know in the light of day. The lunar zodiac shows
that hidden self which our conscious mind only dimly
recognizes, nor has any idea of the powers which lie there
waiting to be unfolded.

The short side of the triangle demonstrates the path
upwards towards this fuller knowledge as the soul learns
the lessons of the elements. They begin with Saturn and

the earth element, showing the discipline needed both for a harmonious life on the physical plane and for the unfoldment of the inner gifts through service to others and to life itself. It ends with Mercury, the messenger of the gods, who gives wings to the soul to lift it into the heart of the Sun. Yet White Eagle teaches that the final soul test, the earth initiation, is the transformation of the earth element from heavy darkness into the eternal beauty of the solar body—in other words, the etherealization of the solid granite into the beauty of the Sun-self. He says there will come a time when the earth itself will be so raised in vibration that it will be invisible to the younger souls of creation, just as we at present cannot see the shining angelic forms of the Brotherhood of Light who move constantly among us, to bless and heal, when we can be responsive to their harmonies.

When the soul has reached the stage where it longs for spiritual understanding and light on the path ahead, it seems likely that the influence of the lunar zodiac, with its magical thirteenth sign, will begin to be more consciously realized.

According to James Vogh's research, Arachne seems to be linked with the constellation of Auriga, the charioteer, whose chief star, Capella, was of such interest to the builders of the ancient stone circles. Because Vogh's research is crucial, it will be helpful to quote it at some length.

As he notes, it seems significant that the winning tapestry, woven by Arachne, contained thirteen pictures symbolizing the lunar zodiac. This is how he describes them (following the version of the story in Ovid):

'1. Jupiter as a Bull seduces Europa. (*Taurus*)
2. Jupiter pursues Asterie. (?)
3. Jupiter seduces Leda, who bears him twins. (*Gemini*)
4. Neptune is disguised as a river god. (*Cancer*)

59

5. Phoebus is dressed in a lion's skin. (*Leo*)
6. Erigone the virgin. (Specifically said to be *Virgo*)
7. Danae weighs gold in her lap. (*Libra*)
8. Jupiter as a spotted snake. (*Scorpio*)
9. Birth of the centaur Chiron. (*Sagittarius*)
10. Neptune, the sea-god, disguised as a ram. (*Capricorn*)
11. Jupiter seduces the daughter of the river. (*Aquarius*)
12. Neptune disguised as a dolphin. (*Pisces*)
13. Apollo disguised as a herdsman. (*Aries*)

'Thirteen signs are here, except that the second is veiled as Asterie ("of the starry sky"). This suggests that the constellation was seen simply as a group of important stars. It also seems to indicate that the Greeks used the twelve-sign zodiac, borrowed from Babylon before they learned of the thirteen signs from the Celts (the "Hyperboreans")....

'Since Arachne wove only twelve constellations plainly in her tapestry, perhaps reserving the thirteenth, "of the starry sky" for herself, it is right to ask whether she is in some sense the origin of the other twelve signs. In other words, is Silver Wheel a model of the great wheel of the Zodiac? Her constellation has exactly twelve stars; it is the only constellation in or near the Ecliptic which has this number. Were these stars in some way taken to represent the Zodiac?

'We can test this by arbitrarily assigning to each star the name of one sign of the Zodiac. We begin logically with Gemini, the sign that follows Arachne at the end that is next to the constellation of the Twins, and end with Taurus, next to the constellation of the Bull. The other signs of course fall in their correct order. When we do this, Capricorn, the Sea-goat, happens to fall upon the star Capella, whose name means "little goat". It is the only star in the entire hemisphere which bears a name even remotely connected with the Goat. Is this a one-in-a-million co-incidence? Could the constellation of the spider be a little

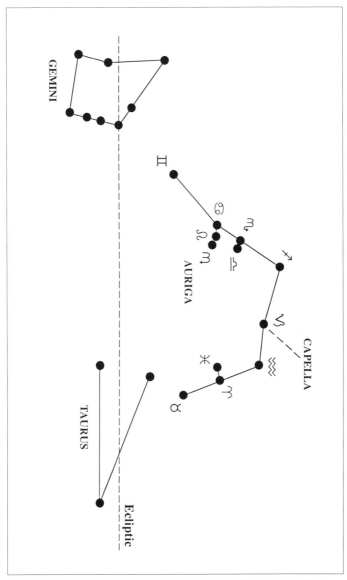

DIAGRAM VIII: THE POSITION OF AURIGA IN THE
HEAVENS, WITH THE LITTLE ZODIAC ILLUSTRATED

wheel "driving" the big wheel of the Zodiac? That is, is it a force connected in some way with the elemental forces of the stars? It may even be called a guide or controller of the Zodiac. The idea may seem remote: we do not expect one sign to affect all of the others. But then ought we to expect a charioteer to control a number of great, plunging, rearing horses—or a spider to control the remote reaches of its web—by means of light cords?'

This idea of the little wheel 'driving' the big wheel of the zodiac seems particularly significant in view of White Eagle's teaching about the law of correspondences and how the little individual has within himself or herself the whole pattern of the Cosmos. 'Man, know thyself, and thou shalt know God and the Universe.' According to the Law of Correspondences, could not the constellation Auriga and its sign Arachne of the lunar zodiac—the Soul zodiac—signify this miniature universe in mankind? The sages of the past who were responsible for building with such precision their stone circles linked with the Sun, Moon and stars, knew the lost secret of how to draw down into the heart of the earth that divine, magical power: a power which holds the stars and planets in their courses and governs the destiny and evolution of worlds beyond our mortal conception.

The evolution of the human soul is carved in stone in the shape of the Sphinx and symbolized in many other legendary creatures which show a human torso on an animal body, such as Oannes the fish god and the Sagittarian centaur. When the soul has progressed from purely physical and animal desires and has also developed to some extent the mental bodies, it reaches the stage of longing for deeper knowledge and wisdom—for light on the path to understanding God and the universe—to progress from the human to the divine man.

At this stage the soul seeks entrance to one of the schools

of inner or mystery teachings—one of the inner brother-hoods associated through the ages with Arachne, where it will be led to its own line of light—its eternal link with the innermost guiding star of its being—its own pole star. This will surely guide it safely through its own labyrinth into the golden world of God. Music-lovers will recognize here the story represented in Mozart's *Magic Flute* where Pamino, holding fast to his true light, is received into the brother-hood of the 'father' Sarastro and enters into a mystical union with his beloved Tamina.

The star Capella, the little goat of the heavens, seems to be linked with Capricorn, the earth sign of the solar zodiac—the solstice sign of Christmas, when the Christ-child, the baby Sun, is born in the cave. Is this why so many of the stone circles were aligned to the star Capella, the chief star of the small zodiac of the human soul, within the lunar (the nurturing mother) zodiac?

Arachne's weaving of the zodiacal tapestry is clearly a symbol of the way in which the soul, through the experi-ences of many lives, learning the lessons and passing the tests of each sign of the zodiac, gradually spins and weaves that wedding garment which prepares her for the mystical marriage—the union of the mortal with the immortal self, which raises the earthly vehicle into eternal life. The lunar goddess Arachne, with her silken thread which drew her up into the heavens, is thought to be another form of the Minoan Greek goddess Ariadne, meaning 'one who spins'. Ariadne also means the most pure—the pure white ether of creation—and again we see symbolized the story of the evolution of the human soul through its many incarnations and various stages of development. As Ariadne gave to Theseus—the hero, the pilgrim soul—that magic silken thread which led him through the labyrinth to slay the monster Minotaur and to emerge triumphant, so the Great Mother gives to each of her children when they enter the labyrinth of earthly experience a magical, pure, silken thread of light. This silk thread keeps them linked with their divine Source through all their struggles with the complexities and frustrations, tests and sorrows of material life, until they finally come to grips with the Minotaur, the lower self, the conquest of which we know as the Second Death. Every soul must learn eventually how to control and transmute the elemental forces of the lower nature.

Since the lunar zodiac birth-chart concerns the inner life of the soul—that aspect of our character which is hidden from others and often inaccessible to our conscious selves—it can be helpful to study it along with the solar zodiac chart, for obviously the solar and lunar parts of our being work together. The meaning of the elements and qualities is the same; the only new factors are the sign Arachne, with its element ether, and the special meaning of the thirteenth house.

We must emphasize that the use of the lunar zodiac in no way invalidates or contradicts the familiar solar chart. Indeed, many people will hardly respond to its more subtle vibrations. When the ordinary solar horoscope is compared with the lunar one, there may be a little change—but sometimes there will be quite a dramatic rearrangement of the sign or house positions of planets, so that the chart is seen in a whole new light. This can provide some interesting new insights, especially with regard to the path of spiritual unfoldment.

The lunar zodiac of thirteen signs needs a similar chart of houses, and the thirteenth house will fall in the part of the horoscope just above the Ascendant, the place of the eastern rising of the sun and planets, which in the solar chart is considered to be the latter part of the twelfth house. The recent statistical researches of Michel Gauqelin have clearly demonstrated the importance of planets placed in this part of the birth-chart and how they surely play a leading part in the life, dominating all other configurations. James Vogh describes this thirteenth house as the 'house of the inner controller', that part of the horoscope which indicates the true work of the inner self and the mission of the soul during the present lifetime.

The words 'inner controller' bring to mind the discoveries of F. M. Alexander, the great exponent of the effect of posture on physical health and mental well-being. After much experimenting on himself (he suffered from an obstinate throat complaint which failed to respond to medical treatment) he discovered that the key-point for controlling the whole bodily posture, and the cure for many health problems, lay at the back of the neck, the shoulders and the top of the spine—the parts ruled by Taurus and Gemini and closely linked with the lungs and breathing. Proper adjustment of this part of the body he called the 'Primary Control', so here perhaps we have the clues, or little pointers as to how this part of the zodiac, the thirteenth house and sign, can affect the whole being.

To look carefully at a planet which falls in the thirteenth house (particularly one close to its cusp) can give a valuable key to an important inner drive or soul mission not necessarily realized in the conscious mind.

A particularly interesting example of major contrasts in the planetary positions in the solar and lunar charts occurs in the case of Prince Albert, consort of Queen Victoria. In the two charts, given here for readers who can interpret a chart, we notice that in the lunar zodiac the Sun and Ascendant move back from Virgo into Leo, while the Moon moves from Scorpio into Libra. The Sun, strong in his own royal sign of Leo, here displaces Mercury as the ruler of the Ascendant, and his position in the thirteenth house shows that, together with Venus, he is the 'inner controller', the key factor in Prince Albert's life. He was truly a king in spirit, yet on the outer plane was the loyal

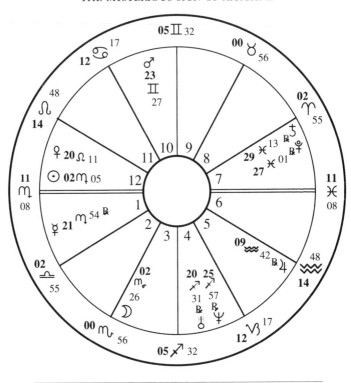

DIAGRAM IX: ALBERT PRINCE CONSORT
(SOLAR CHART)

AUGUST 26th 1819: 6.08 AM GMT
COBURG, GERMANY: 50N15 : 10E58
TOPOCENTRIC HOUSES

server (Virgo) of his beloved wife. The position of Venus in Leo in the thirteenth house is also significant. In this lunar chart the Moon has moved into Libra, making Venus ruler of the Moon's sign. Also, Taurus, the other sign of Venus, is on the cusp of the tenth house, which signifies the profession. The angular distances between the planets—the aspects—are the same in both charts. In a man's birth-

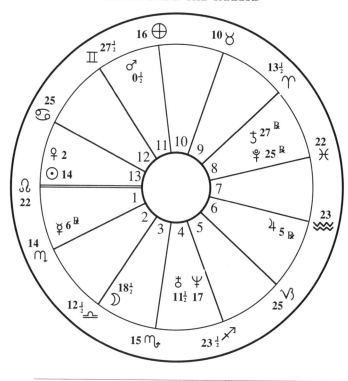

DIAGRAM X: ALBERT PRINCE CONSORT
(LUNAR CHART)

AUGUST 26th 1819: 6.08 AM GMT
COBURG, GERMANY: 50N15 : 10E58
TOPOCENTRIC HOUSES

chart the Moon signifies the wife, and here she is in Libra, the sign of partnership and marriage, and Venus governs the tenth house of the career. Does not this planetary balance on the inner, or soul plane, show most clearly Prince Albert's destiny? He had all the capabilities of a true monarch, and his Sun in the fiery Leo shows him learning the inner, soul lesson of love—sacrificial love. But its

67

position in Virgo in the solar chart shows how his deep love was expressed in service to his beloved Queen-wife and her subjects.

During his life of devoted service, he became undoubtedly the power behind the throne—a fact which was more fully recognized after his death. He thus demonstrated a basic principle of Arachne as the 'little wheel behind the scenes, driving the big wheel of the state'.

6

SATURN AND THE BLUEPRINT OF SPIRITUAL UNFOLDMENT

THE ROOT CHAKRA, as we have said, is principally saturnian, and associated with the earliest stages of soul growth, as it is with the physical growth of the babe in the womb. During the first month of gestation, the little heart starts to beat and grow stronger, while the skeletal structure begins to take form. Saturn and the Sun between them rule the heart and the bony framework of the body, especially the spine, the channel for the spinal cord, from which springs the main nerves of the body.

Saturn, the polar opposite of the Sun and Moon (symbols of the eternal self of the spirit and the present earthly personality) holds the blueprint—the basic plan, the karma—of each incarnation, just as he is responsible for the skeleton which supports the body and also the skin—its outermost limit. In occult philosophy the different sections of the spine have their own significance in the development of the solar body. They are linked with the chakras, or energy-centres in the etheric body which are concerned with the growth and development of the subtler vehicles which will enable the soul to function freely on all the different planes of consciousness—from the physical right through to the celestial.

The wonderful allegorical pictures in the Revelation of St John are concerned, White Eagle says, more with the inner soul experiences and tests which come as these energy-centres are awakened than with dire prophecies about the end of the world. The end of the world, he says, means the end of the soul's sojourn in the lower planes of its own selfish limitations, which he describes as 'the Second Death'.

The spine has thirty-three segments, or vertebrae, a number which seems to have occult significance. Jesus lived for thirty-three years; David reigned for thirty-three years; in Freemasonry there are thirty-three degrees of enlightenment or initiation. In occult philosophy the spine is said to represent the straight and narrow way which leads to freedom and spiritual mastery, a Jacob's ladder between heaven and earth.

The number of bones in each of the five different sections of the spine seems to have significance in the divine plan for the building of the solar body, a blue-print for the temple of the New Jerusalem(see table overleaf). The fourteen bones of the lower spine are linked with the lower chakras and concerned with the development of physical skills and mastery of the environment. They mark the first stage of the awakening God-consciousness, training the soul to make use of all the materials of its environment to create better living conditions, to live peacefully in communities, and to unfold the physical and mental qualities which are part of civilization.

The number fourteen also has occult significance. In the Egyptian Mysteries, for instance, the body of the slain Osiris was cut up into fourteen pieces and scattered about the land of Egypt. These pieces were gradually found and gathered together by Isis (symbol of the Moon, the divine Mother) to be healed and resurrected as the arisen God of the Sun.

White Eagle, in one of his inner teachings, has told us that in occult philosophy the body with all its pleasures and indulgences was often referred to as 'the land of Egypt';

holding the soul in bondage from which the Israelites (the children of Ra, children of the Sun) had eventually to free themselves. The symbol of the lowest chakra is the four-petalled lotus making the square (or cross); and it shows the imprisonment, within matter—in the inertia of the earthy signs—of the golden seed, the solar fire, which must be awakened and gradually drawn up the spine to vitalize each chakra and illumine the soul on every plane of being. It is interesting that the lowest part of the spine, the coccyx, has four bones fused together.

After the four bones of the coccyx we come to the two sets of five vertebrae in the lumbar and sacral region. The two sets of five remind us of the Ten Commandments, the laws of conduct for the 'Children of Israel' (the Children of the Sun, Ra) given to Moses when he led them out of the land of Egypt; and the five *yamas* and *niyamas* of Patanjali, the great disciplines, which form the first stages in the training of the yogi.

The *yamas* and *niyamas* are more fully described in YOGA OF THE HEART by Jenny Beeken, a companion to the present volume, so here we just give a brief summary. Each one takes on a deeper meaning as we ponder upon it, for these disciplines are relevant on every plane of being, from the physical right through to the higher mental and celestial. They are the first essential steps of the spiritual quest which leads to the transformation from the human into the divine consciousness.

The *yamas* are the universal, moral principles of: 1) non-violence; 2) truth; 3) non-stealing; 4) celibacy*; and 5) non-possessiveness (similar to the last five commandments in the Bible).

The *niyamas* grow from the constant effort to observe

---

* This word is the usual translation of the Sanskrit. The phrase Jenny uses, 'reverence for the creative life-force within', perhaps better describes the meaning.

DIAGRAM X: THE SPINE
Symbol of the straight and narrow path of
human development

The Crown SAHASRARA Cosmic Consciousness

STAGE FOUR:

THE HEAD CENTRES
The Brow ✹ (*ajna*)
The Top of the Forehead ✹ (*lalata*)
The Centre of the Brain ✹ (*soma*)

When thinking of the centres in the head, it is easy to confuse the frontal mind with the awakening of the inner vision and the unfoldment of cosmic awareness which is the true function of these centres. The illumination of consciousness associated with the crown chakra, known as the blooming of the thousand-petalled lotus—*sahasrara*—right above the physical skull (the halo) is the culmination, the blending, of the energies of all the other chakras when they have been brought fully into action and are perfectly balanced. This is the ultimate aim of the pilgrim on the spiritual path: to find that union with the divine mind which dissolves all sense of separateness. It is the aim and end of all spiritual training.

STAGE THREE:
AWARENESS OF
CELESTIAL WORLD.
7 Cervical (neck) verte-
brae linked with the seven
planets and the more
advanced stage of spiritual
unfoldment along the
different planetary rays.

✹
●
●
●
●
●
●
●
●

THROAT
(*VISUDDHA*)
CHAKRA

Element: Ether
Quality: Mutable
Sense: Hearing

STAGE TWO	✪	HEART (*ANAHATA*)
AWARENESS OF SOUL	●	CHAKRA
WORLD—ASTRAL AND	●	Element: Air
MENTAL PLANES.	●	Mode or Quality: Fixed
	●	Sense: Feeling and Touch
	●	
12 thoracic (chest) verte-	●	
brae to which ribs are att-	●	
ached, protecting heart and	●	when the soul has con-
lungs. Linked with the	●	sciously started treading
twelve signs of the zodiac	●	'the Path' to spiritual
and the soul lessons of the	●	freedom and enlighten-
elements, to be learnt	●	ment.

THE DIAPHRAGM

STAGE ONE		
AWARENESS OF PHYSI-	✪	SOLAR PLEXUS
CAL & ETHERIC WORLD.	●	(*MANIPURAKA* AND
5 lumbar vertebrae: the	●	*SURYA* CHAKRAS)
astral or desire body—am-	●	Element: Fire
bition, enthusiasm, energy,	●	Mode or Quality: Cardinal
fiery loves and hates.	●	Sense: Sight
5 sacral vertebrae: the	✪	SACRAL (*SVADHIS-*
etheric body, mortal and	●	*THANA*) CHAKRA
immortal—psychic, recep-	●	Element: Water
tive creativity on all	●	Mode or Quality: Mutable
planes. The great ocean of	●	Sense: Taste
etheric life.	●	
4 coccyx vertebrae: the	✪	ROOT (*MULADHARA*)
physical world and all that	●	CHAKRA
pertains to it. Diet and	●	Element: Earth
digestion, excretion of	●	Mode or Quality: Fixed
waste.	●	Sense: Smell

BASE OF SPINE

these principles in daily life. They are: 1) purity (of body, mind and heart); 2) contentment and tranquillity; 3) fortitude and enthusiasm; 4) self-awareness—'Man, know thyself and thou shalt know God and the Universe'; 5) dedication to God of all one's thoughts and actions. The will to will the will of God.

The number five seems to be significant in our physical make-up, with our five senses, five groups of vertebrae, and five fingers and toes. They can be a constant reminder of the five great laws which govern human life.

Five is the number of the planet Mercury, the Messenger of the Gods, and closest of all to the Sun. The subtler vibrations of this planet are far beyond the understanding of most of us at the present time, but its influence awakens us eventually to fully conscious realization of our union with the universal Sun, the Cosmic Christ. Then the mind of God will shine through the human consciousness and every cell of that glorious human and solar body, keeping it eternally young, strong and full of joy.

In Hindu tradition each chakra is given its own mandala, which is based on the circle, indicating the vortex of energy which it represents. This vortex of energy arises not from the physical spinal cord, but from its counterpart in the etheric body (that subtler body which closely interpenetrates the physical). Seen clairvoyantly, in a spiritually developed soul, the chakras look rather like flowers vibrating with light and colour, growing from the etheric spinal cord. The greater the degree of spiritual awakening through selfless love and service (not through exercises centred solely on the self, or much reading!), the more these 'flowers' glow and vibrate with light and colour, enveloping with a healing peace all who come within the aura of such a soul. On the other hand, the chakras in one who is as yet spiritually unawakened may just appear as dully glowing discs.

In the mandalas each chakra is depicted as a circle containing a lotus flower with a different number of petals, the number of petals having its own significance. Each chakra is also associated with a male and female goddess and an animal symbol. Astrologically, each chakra has an element associated with it: and to each element there are three zodiacal signs. Many of these signs are based on animals, while their rulers are the planetary gods and goddesses familiar in Roman, Greek and Egyptian symbolism. In considering the influence of the dominant planet concerned with each chakra, we also find a link by polarity with the ruler of the opposite sign—that is, Saturn with the Sun and Moon, Jupiter with Mercury, and Mars with Venus, a polarity similar to the two gods of eastern symbology.

Another interesting truth is demonstrated by the animal associated with the chakra (which we shall describe in due course). Such symbolism emphasizes the vital importance of a healthy and strong physical or animal life, upon which foundation first the human values develop, and then the divine. In the Egyptian tradition the same pattern occurs in the Sphinx, whose human torso arises out of the animal body. Symbols such as this are common in Graeco-Roman mythology too. Some classical statues and monuments are given wings, indicating the divine self growing out of the human consciousness.

The chakras are commonly regarded as forming two triangles, which are separated from each other by the diaphragm, that umbrella-shaped muscle which is so important in the regulation of the breathing. Yogis regard this as a bridge between the outer and the inner body—the physical and the soul life. The upper triangle, the major and minor chakras connected with the heart, the throat and the head, are concerned with spiritual awakening and the unfoldment of the subtler vehicles which come under the influence of those planets so close to the Sun, namely Venus and Mercury. The three chakras below the diaphragm are known as the lower or basic triangle, the triangle of earthly life and of personal desire and aspiration.

Mediaeval philosophers regarded the part of the physical body below the diaphragm as connected with the elemental world, full of stormy emotion and conflict, or like a muddy bog, almost suffocating the soul under a weight of depression and responsibility. Earth and water make mud. Fire and water make steam. But all create motive power for soul growth. The many coils of the digestive tract which are associated with this lower triangle may well be symbolized in the mystical labyrinths, which seem to have almost universal occult significance. The struggles of the soul with the desires, emotions and appetites of the lower self are pictured in the deadly fight of the hero Theseus with the Minotaur at the heart of the labyrinth. It is interesting that the fire and water signs are paired by their planetary rulers Mars, Jupiter and the Sun–Moon, the Sun being the positive ruler of his own sign Leo, and the Moon of the negative watery Cancer. Both are polarized with Saturn, ruler of earthy Capricorn and airy Aquarius.

Above the diaphragm, the first chakra is that of the heart, associated with the air element and thus the signs Libra, Gemini and Aquarius. Among these three signs, unlike those of the lower chakras, the lack of an animal symbol is conspicuous, although the eastern mandala has the black antelope, swift-footed and restless. Libra (the scales in which the soul is weighed at the end of each incarnation) seems to be linked with the Egyptian mysteries in which the soul is weighed in the scales. Perhaps the delicate adjustment of the scales to record even a feather's weight can be compared with the lightning-swift movements of the antelope. The two human symbols among the air signs, namely Gemini, the heavenly twins, and Aquarius, the man with the water-pot, lead the soul eventually to the fountain of eternal life.

Saturn's exaltation in the Venus sign of Libra, shows how he holds the scales of judgment; and the principle of judgment is always the same—how far we have obeyed the two great commandments, to which Jesus said that all spiritual law could be reduced:

Thou shalt love the Lord thy God with all thy heart, and with all thy soul, and with all thy mind, and with all thy strength, and *Thou shalt love thy neighbour as thyself.* (Mark 12:30-31).

White Eagle, in THE LIVING WORD OF ST JOHN, has expounded this very beautifully:

'Immediately man's spirit goes forth in adoration to God, his heart subtly contacts the rest of all creation, particularly the human creation. He realizes in a flash his at-one-ment with God. He knows that if God is in himself, God is also in his brother man. If man finds God in the holy of holies within his own soul, he knows without being preached at that his fellow man has been created in the same way as himself, and shares in the same holy light. Even if it is unawakened, it is still there, waiting. And he knows that by giving out love to his neighbour he is not only helping his neighbour to deal with practical problems of daily life, but also to awaken to the eternal God-consciousness within him.'

Deep in every heart, the recording angels of Mercury (Gemini) and Saturn (Aquarius) keep strict account of how far the lower self has accepted and tried to live by these two simple laws of love; and when, after a period of rest and refreshment in the higher worlds, the soul returns for another day of earth life, it is this heart record which shows the special lesson which needs to be absorbed.

In the birth-chart, the Sun (ruler of the physical heart)

represents not only the earthly father but also that individual spirit which is descending from the higher worlds for a period of work and experience on the physical plane. White Eagle teaches that the position of the Sun in the signs of the zodiac always gives a pointer as to the deep inner lesson which the soul has come to learn: the true purpose of the incarnation. The Moon in every chart represents the mother, both the divine Mother and the earthly mother, and also that feminine aspect of the soul which—through the everyday experience and the emotional reaction to all the happenings of daily life, particularly in the family—is gathering materials for the building of the eternal Soul Temple, again represented by the Moon.

Saturn shows the path of discipline the soul has chosen: through the earth signs, teaching patience, endurance and the acceptance of responsibility; through the water signs, teaching discipline of the emotions, possibly through frustrations in the feeling side of the nature, or heavy family responsibility; through the fire signs, disciplining the intensely eager aspirations and ambitions for selfish ends into devotion and sacrificial love; and through the air signs, teaching discipline of the mind and wise direction of thought power to create harmony and beauty in the life. In horoscope interpretation, differences in the zodiacal sign of the Sun, Moon and Saturn in the solar and the lunar charts can give indications of deeper soul lessons being learnt, or special karmic conditions. The comparison of the two can be most interesting and helpful.

The symbolism of astrology can lead us to an understanding of those universal spiritual truths which teachers and seers throughout the ages have tried to express, in parables, myths and legends, according to the needs of their own particular race and age.

Although during each incarnation the soul's energies

may be specially focused on the development of one or other of the subtler bodies, this does not preclude the use and continued growth of those already in being. A plant or tree does not stop growing new leaves and shoots, or extending its root system, because a flower bud is forming; there will still be general growth, but with an extra concentration of energy on the flower. Sometimes, however, a soul before coming into incarnation may realize and accept the necessity of blocking off certain faculties which perhaps have been over-developed in the past, in order to make it work harder on another aspect of being which needs to be brought into fuller manifestation. In such a case the soul comes back inhibited in its personality in some way, either in its emotions, or in its mind or body. This is why it is foolish for anyone to judge or condemn the actions of another, for we do not know the special task which that soul has set itself, nor the inner tests and trials it is meeting. The purpose of continued incarnation is to bring about the perfect balance, the union of the two triangles, the mystical marriage.

White Eagle says:

'The mystical marriage between the Lamb and God signifies or symbolizes the union between the collective Soul of Man, its path of earth-experience fulfilled; and the Spirit, or God; between the perfected One, the Lamb, which shall be arrayed as the Bride in that "fine linen which is as the righteousness of saints," with the Bridegroom, or Spirit of God. Translating this from the macrocosm to the microcosm, from the general to the particular, here is another reference to the transmutation of the life-giving or creative centres, their merging or marriage with the higher centres of throat and heart and head....

'Following the mystical marriage, or the salvation of one Cycle—the great Return—the powers of Evil lie in abeyance for a time, their task accomplished; and the souls of the freed go forth to glory far outside our conception; therein they rest, enjoy the fruits of their harvest, await the summons and the challenge of some high and new adventure.'

7

THE *MULADHARA* (ROOT) CHAKRA
AND THE EARTH ELEMENT

IN THE FOLLOWING chapters, which describe the functions of the different chakras, we are trying to show how our daily life-experience and spiritual aspiration can help to bring into harmonious action the cosmic energies, the life-force of these psychic centres; which, flowing through the aura, will bring increased health and vitality to body and mind, and create increasing harmony in the whole life.

The element of each chakra, with its three modes of expression, and the planetary rulers of the signs involved, naturally manifest as our mental and emotional outlook, our physical health, and lifestyle. In describing the action of these signs and planets we are trying to show how to use wisely the tools which they give to build in all its beauty the eternal Soul Temple, the foundations of which have to be firmly based on the daily experiences of life on earth.

With the root chakra, Saturn and the Moon (its polar opposite) are both specially significant, indicating the drawing down into earthly incarnation of the virgin soul, daughter of the divine Mother and always under her protection.

Mars, which is exalted in Capricorn, is also represented. All these planets are concerned with the creation of a new physical body; but Saturn, ruler of Capricorn, is the dominant factor, giving the blueprint of the opportunities, the limitations and the burdens of the life ahead which are going to help the soul to climb to the top of the mountain.

It is interesting, too, that Mars, planet of solar fire and energy, should be exalted in Capricorn, for locked in this earth centre is the solar fire of *kundalini*, which lies dormant until a certain stage of soul experience has been reached. Then it begins to rise up the spine, awakening and energizing in turn each of the chakras, until they are all vibrating with glorious light, sound and colour.

In the East there is much knowledge and experience of this *kundalini* fire and many different methods of helping it to be drawn up. It is important to remember that the eastern mind and physical constitution differs somewhat from that of the West. Methods suitable for students in India and Tibet need adapting for the western mind and body. Safer for the Westerner is the training which comes chiefly through action and practical service—learning to work in harmony with natural law; learning to obey the laws of health and harmonious living. As this becomes a habitual way of life and as the soul aspires heavenwards, there will come a gradual, safe and healthy stimulation of this solar fire, until it illumines each of the chakras and the whole body radiates this divine energy and beauty.

THE *MULADHARA* (ROOT) CHAKRA

Soul Lesson: Service
Element: Earth
Sense: Smell
Lotus symbol: Four petals

The three earth signs are Capricorn, the goat; Taurus, the bull; and (the one human sign) Virgo, the virgin. In the traditional mandala, the animal associated with this chakra is the elephant. It is interesting that so many of the most powerful creatures on the earth are herbivores, those who quietly chew and re-chew the grass of earth life. The bull, the elephant and the horse, so-called 'beasts of burden', have been used through the ages in the service of man for all kinds of heavy work. This phrase illustrates the spiritual lesson of the earth signs: service on every plane, from the coarsest, heaviest work in and on the earth, to the eventual perfection of the solar body through the giving of love— the completion of the Soul Temple in which the Christ Sun shines in its full glory.

The root chakra is particularly concerned with the physical body, its needs and maintenance, and with the practicalities of life. People with a strong balance of planets in earth signs tend to be realists, down-to-earth people, well able to organize and create harmonious conditions in homes, in businesses, in estate management, and are involved in any kind of activity concerned with bringing comfort and order and method into physical life.

Let us now look at the three earth signs in detail:

The Sun passes through the cardinal earth sign of Capricorn between 22nd December and 21st January.* Saturn, ruler of Capricorn, is, according to the traditional planetary order, the 'planetary god' of the root chakra, while his polar opposite the Moon, ruler of Cancer, is associated with the centre in the head which in Hindu symbolism eventually flowers as the 'thousand-petalled lotus', or in Christian tradition becomes the bride of Christ, the 'woman clothed with the Sun'.

Both Capricorn and Cancer are concerned with family life, their houses in the horoscope signifying the basic structure of the life, parentage, home, and the conditions for worldly service and success. In each incarnation the

*The dates given here and hereafter are for a typical year. They do in fact vary slightly, between the 20th and 24th of the month (19th in the case of February)

higher self makes the link with the physical plane through the will of Saturn, the perfectionist, drawing it down to earth. Under the guidance of this great soul teacher it will have chosen the life conditions which will give opportunities for perfecting the eternal Soul Temple which it is building in the heavens. Capricorn and the tenth house of the horoscope signify the father, or dominant parent, the employer, and the worldly position which can be attained, depending upon the discipline and will-power of the native and the karmic opportunities which are presented.

In India, a nation strongly under Capricorn, a rigid caste system allocating social position by birth has held sway for thousands of years. With the dawn of the Aquarian age, this is now gradually disintegrating; but in earlier centuries it was believed that souls, as they learned their lessons and made the most of their opportunities, would pass to the next sphere of service in the caste system above them. Progress in the social sphere was linked with the spiritual unfoldment of the soul, and formed an orderly pattern.

This idea of progress according to a precise and orderly pattern is part of the capricornian temperament. Souls born under this sign have the practicality of the earth element, and—like the mountain goat which is their symbol—they also have a keen ambition to reach the peak of the particular mountain which is their sphere of attainment. Saturn, ruler of the sign, gives an indomitable will-power and determination to achieve its aims, together with a practical understanding of the difficulties and obstacles to be overcome. Souls in whom this influence can manifest freely, and at its finest level, will work hard and unceasingly in the service of the community. They do not hurry or look for short cuts, for they realize the need to build on a firm and precise foundation; or, in masonic language, to 'build on the square' at every level of their being, for Saturn requires precision and perfection in its manifestation. They can be such perfectionists and so determined in pursuing their ends that they become stern and ruthless task-masters, both to themselves and to those under their jurisdiction. They make hard, but usually just, managers, employers and teachers, expecting the best from their workers and students.

Capricornians, being such perfectionists, can be miserly in their praise and somewhat stingy in their recompense to those who serve them, for they are by nature economical and careful. This is largely due to fear of the future, and the possibility of having to depend on others for their needs. To the proud, independent spirit this would be an intolerable situation. The true child of Saturn finds it difficult to ask for help, or metaphorically to go down on their knees! The planet of limitation, crystallization and consolidation, Saturn sets the limits through which the soul must work. Through Capricorn he governs the skin—the outer limit of the physical body, and also the bony structure, especially the knees—symbolic perhaps of the soul's need to learn to kneel and pray for the guidance and help of God. Rigid independence and pride of self-will can be a great stumbling block, which can manifest in troubles such as arthritis (especially in the knees).

The Sun passes through the fixed earth sign of Taurus between 20th April and 21st May (solar zodiac) or 18th April and 16th May (lunar zodiac). Taurus gives a quiet, steady, tenacious temperament, easy-going but very determined and persistent. Venus, its ruling planet, brings warmth and kindness to the nature, although in this case with a degree of possessiveness in the affections, particularly where the family are involved, for Taurus is linked with the second house of the birth-chart, governing finances and possessions, both physical and emotional.

The quiet practicality and methodical working habits of Taureans give them the capacity for building not only with bricks and mortar, but also for creating an organization, building up a farm or estate, a business, an altruistic enterprise, or an artistic career; building up a collection of antiques, pictures, stamps or other objects which can grow in value. The business sense of a Taurean is usually sound, unless Venus is badly placed and aspected. Through this earth sign, Venus stimulates a natural desire for physical comfort; good food, pleasure, luxury and harmonious surroundings, together with the financial security which makes this possible. Many Taureans find themselves working in banks, accountancy or business projects in which they are responsible for money and possessions. Earthly security is particularly important to them and lessons have to be learned through money and possessions or the lack of them. Every soul needs to discover through contrasting experiences of wealth and poverty the true place in life of money and possessions, and how to become attuned to that steady flow of sustenance on all planes which comes through loving service to life and trust in divine providence. Wise use of wealth and power is an important soul lesson of the earth element and the successful businessman or woman who provides valuable employment and is conscientiously responsible for the well-being of many people, is giving valuable spiritual service and working in harmony with divine law.

Physically Taurus rules the throat, the thyroid gland and the vocal chords, and often gives its subjects a good singing or speaking voice. There will always be an appreciation of beauty, particularly in music and sound—sound which can have such a powerful effect, not only on the physical, but the subtler planes of being. Taurus also gives an appreciation of ritual and ceremonial which creates form on the etheric plane. The practical, earthy mind of Taureans sometimes makes it difficult for them to meditate solely by visualizing an opening rose or a lotus pool, but their consciousness can be raised with the help of music, ritual and ceremonial, or perhaps a statue, picture, or some other physical object which appeals to their sense of beauty and enables them to open their hearts to the beauty of the inner worlds. Flowers, trees and natural scenes are healing and inspiring, and indeed many souls working on the earth lesson feel 'closer to God in a garden', working with the earth and with growing plants, than when trying to meditate on abstract ideas. Since the earth element is associated with the sense of smell, souls with this element emphasized will find that the fragrance of the incense in ritual, or of a lovely open flower, will help to awaken their awareness of the inner world. Part of their spiritual unfoldment and awareness of inner truth will come through purity of diet, and attunement with nature and the harmonious, rhythmic pattern of life.

The exaltation of the Moon, symbol of the divine Mother and also of the individual soul, in this fixed earth sign, is a reminder once again that the purpose of every incarnation is the gradual building of the eternal Soul Temple. In Taurus the essential restlessness of the Moon is steadied and her creative powers developed under the influence of the angels of Venus, angels of harmony and beauty.

Between 23rd August and 23rd September the Sun passes through the mutable sign of Virgo, the most subtle and flexible of the earth signs. In the lunar zodiac, the dates become 5th September and 3rd October. Mercury is exalted here, indicating how this messenger of the Sun will bring to the soul the discrimination and wisdom which will enable it eventually to transform the coarser cells of the physical body into that pure, vibrant and completely healthy illumined body which the great masters and teachers create for their work with humanity. Their bodies have become beautiful, perfected temples of the spirit, vehicles through which the life-force and healing power of the Sun can flow, unhindered by any trace of self-will. The masters and adepts live constantly in this cosmic consciousness, their lesser selves united with the great Sun. This is the union with the eternal self which all yogis seek.

Virgo is the sign of the alchemist, striving to transmute the base metal of the lower self (lead, ruled by Saturn, which weighs the soul down to the earth) into the pure gold of the Sun-consciousness which unites us with God and with all life.

Virgo is linked with the sixth house of the horoscope, connected with health and healing and also with service or employment.

In Virgo we may see the principle of service expressed in its purest and most beautiful form. Many of the devoted servants of humanity—doctors, nurses, healers, carers of all kinds—come under this sign, which is also connected with diet and with all natural forms of healing.

Mercurial people need to use their hands in the expression of their ideas and soul energy. This may well come in some artistic form such as playing a musical instrument, in painting, writing, in draughtsmanship and design, or in work which calls for flexible manual control, but most frequently it will manifest in some form of healing—physiotherapy, massage or even surgery.

Because Mercury activates the mind, his subjects are usually studious. They have a natural feeling for precision in detail, and a desire for perfection which not only helps their concentration and interest in their work, but also intensifies their critical faculties to such an extent that they may suffer from a worrying sense of inadequacy. In their struggle for perfection they often feel defeated by the impossibility of achieving in practical life the ideals which they can see in their minds. For this reason they often find life more harmonious when they can work under the direction of a master or an employer who will guide their service and take ultimate responsibility for the result. They thus make capable, reliable and devoted secretaries and personal assistants, because of their grasp of practical detail which, with training and discipline, makes them invaluable in the organization of any enterprise. Since Virgo governs the bowels and digestive tract her subjects can easily become nervously depleted through worry and anxiety, which causes digestive disorders. They need to guard against over-conscientiousness and too much seeking after perfection.

Mercury, the planet of the mind, helps the soul to develop the power of reason and logic, thought and invention, and thereby gradually acquire the wisdom and discrimination needed to control and manipulate coarse physical matter. White Eagle has said that when the soul comes onto the physical plane to gain experience, the life ahead is like an unploughed field, and he or she has to learn how to bring that field into a state of harmony and beauty through thought, planning and hard work—thus learning to function in harmony with the great laws of life. The exaltation of Mercury in this his own sign, the sign of humility, purity and perfection—of selfless service—and also of health, shows how the alchemy of pure heavenly communion will ultimately transform and illumine every cell of the body.

Virgo symbolizes the soul as the virgin, purified and illumined by the divine love which shines through every act of service, and asking for no reward except the joy of bringing harmony and beauty into every aspect of life. This selfless service gradually weaves her wedding garment.

The importance of the root—*muladhara*—chakra in the building of the Soul Temple is clearly indicated by the number of planets involved either as rulers of the earth signs, as therefore exalted therein, or in polarity through ruling the opposite sign. But ultimately the planet of this chakra is Saturn, who governs the latter part of life when all the thoughts, actions and emotional experiences of the past years begin clearly to manifest in the physical body.

Most of us, as we grow older, find our bodies increasingly afflicted by stiffness, pain and discomfort and many minor trials which restrict movement and increasingly limit our ability to achieve all that we want to do. People coming strongly under the Saturn signs are particularly likely to feel his disciplinary powers in some way, forcing them to learn lessons of patience and perseverance or to accept karmic responsibilities to the best of their ability. Saturn tends to give them a somewhat pessimistic outlook, which they call realistic, but which causes them much unnecessary worry, fear and anxiety about the future. With Aquarians this can cause nervous strain and tension which prevents the natural flowing of the life-forces of joy and vitality, a restriction which may manifest in the body such as stiffness in the knees and other joints, rheumatic and arthritic troubles, or in severe cramps or circulatory troubles—complaints which impede people in activities they enjoy and, again, become a severe test of patience.

To encourage a feeling of the life-force flowing freely through the body, it can be helpful to relax whenever possible, sitting on a table or a high stool which allows the lower legs and feet to swing from the knees freely and easily, and try to feel all mental tension and strain relaxing with the easy movements. Hold the spine straight but not stiff while doing this, and at the same time attune yourself to the gentle flow of the breath. For those who can easily lie flat on the floor, another way to encourage flexibility in the knee joints is by gentle, rhythmic, cycling movements, trying to keep the spine flat and relaxed. This movement should not be an absent-minded rush, but gentle, peaceful and rhythmic, with quiet easy breathing, keeping the mind aware of a golden light flowing into the knees, hips and feet. There should be no sense of strain. Only do as many cycles as can easily be managed, gradually working up to about fifty.

The frustrations of old age are due to the accumulation of the personal habits of thought and lifestyle which build up over the years to form a crust almost like a hard shell, through which the joyful vitality of the higher self can penetrate less easily. These habitual thought-patterns can, in old age, close in the soul so powerfully that loved ones in close attendance can scarcely recognize the real self of the one they love. This is the 'body elemental', the weight of saturnian lead holding down the soul which is longing to escape to freedom.

Once we become aware of the tendency these habits of the lower self have to crystallize or form a crust, it is possible for all of us to take steps to remain flexible in body and mind: to try and relinquish gracefully conditions in our lives which have become outworn; and to use creative thought-power to learn more of the mystery of life and death and to build a bridge between the inner and the outer life.

On the physical plane it is helpful to watch the diet, ensuring that the food taken is full of vitality. This should not be difficult nowadays when there is so much emphasis on wholefoods, foods full of the life-force of the earth, which are best eaten raw when possible. It is important as we grow older to strengthen and purify the body with vitalizing food. There is now a huge choice of systems of exercise designed to keep the body flexible too, although— and this is especially true for the Saturn subject—gentle but persistent movements are best. In yoga especially we can find exercises which involve a relaxed awareness of the way the different parts of the body function; so that we can bring our thought-power into every movement, realizing gradually how the different parts of our body affect both mind and emotions. This helps us to become more aware of how we become over-tense in our desire for achievement. Through quiet breathing we can learn to relax that fierce grip of the body, to unclench the teeth, to let the shoulders relax loosely downwards, so that the heart is free and open to receive the divine Breath.

This will bring increasingly a sense of peaceful acceptance and serenity of spirit. Truly we begin to build the bridge between the two worlds and look forward to reunion with those we love in the world of light. The reality of eternal life dawns ever more clearly as we learn to look backwards with thankfulness and forward with hope—and with the assurance that love is eternal.

8

THE *SVADHISTHANA* (SACRAL) CHAKRA
AND THE WATER ELEMENT

Soul Lesson: Peace and Wisdom
Element: Water
Sense: Taste
Lotus symbol: Six petals

THE NEXT CHAKRA above the *muladhara* is *svadhisthana*, the sacral chakra, which governs the sense of taste, and is associated with the three water signs—Pisces, Cancer and Scorpio, ruled by Jupiter, the Moon and Mars respectively.

Jupiter, the next in the traditional planetary order, has a particularly close association with the water element, since he not only rules Pisces but is exalted in Cancer—the water sign ruled by the Moon, symbol of the divine Mother, the creator of continually changing forms through which the Christ spirit, the Sun, can manifest in matter. In the symbol for this chakra, the animal is the alligator, strong and virile, lurking in the water to seize upon its unwary prey. The sacral chakra is closely involved with the etheric body and those hidden creative powers within the human soul which spring from the great ocean of cosmic consciousness, and build form on every plane of life.

The physical body and personality of the lower self is recreated with each new incarnation, just as a tree puts forth fresh growth every spring; but the subtler vehicles, which are gradually developed through the experiences of physical life, may be likened to the trunk and branches of the tree which steadily grows taller and stronger, while the roots penetrate more deeply into mother earth for her sustaining nourishment. The fresh leaves of each new incarnation absorb the sunlight—the energy of the eternal Heavenly Father—which is drawn down through the branches and the trunk to the roots; while the roots draw nourishment from the earth and send the sap upwards to promote new growth.

When the time has come for the soul once more to return into physical incarnation, it is most lovingly enfolded in the care and protection of the divine Mother. Her wisdom guides it to the choice of experience for this, the next 'day' of life. The Moon is the instrument of the divine Mother for the building of the vehicles required by the soul for its life in earthly matter. At the time which is right for the planetary builders to fulfil the plan of the Great Architect, a powerful ray from the spiritual Sun energizes the permanent atom, that centre or seed deep within the soul which holds the residue, the record, of all past lives. Then the divine Mother, with her angelic throng, sets to work with the energized seed, building the vehicles which will enable the incarnating soul to function on the different planes of being according to the opportunities and limitations allowed by the past karma. The will of the Heavenly Father, architect of the Soul Temple, shines through the earthly parents, guiding the angelic builders to gather the materials for the mental, astral and etheric bodies which the soul needs.

The symbol of the alligator lurking in the water, watching for his unwary prey, illustrates the formidable power of the water element, which is linked with the generative organs and with creative activity on the etheric plane through the power of thought and imagination—creation which can be heavenly or diabolical.

The earth element holds a seed firmly under the ground, but when it is watered and the outside husk breaks, there comes rapid growth and expansion into the freedom of the open air. Jupiter is concerned with this principle of growth and expansion, and the flow of the life-force through the whole being. Jupiter (ruler of Pisces) and Mars (ruler of Scorpio) bring tremendous psychic energy to this chakra. Scorpio is concerned with death and the inner world—the afterlife. The Moon, ruler of Cancer, who presides over the building and destruction of form, has her fall in Scorpio.

Pisces, the sign through which the Sun passes between 19th February and 20th March, is the exaltation sign of Venus, the polar opposite of Mars. Here the water element, in its mutable quality, symbolizes that great ocean of divine life and consciousness in which we all have our being. The symbol of Pisces, the two fishes bound together but facing in opposite directions, demonstrates the duality of this sign, and how souls strongly under its influence are aware, often unconsciously, not only of the outer physical life, but also of that etheric soul world which interpenetrates it. They reflect almost instantly the thoughts and feelings of people with whom they come into contact, and may find difficulty in distinguishing between their own moods and reactions, and those which they absorb from their surroundings. On entering a room or a building they may feel a vivid impression of the etheric memories of the place—sensing events that have happened there, either recently or in the past.

Jupiter is traditionally known as the 'greater benefic', being the planet of growth and expansion on all planes, but he is especially concerned with the unfoldment of the higher mind. Jupiter and Pisces both give a yearning towards religious and philosophical experience and the unity of spirit which can build up in a gathering of souls for communal prayer and worship. In such gatherings, the mystical ceremony of communion, with its symbols of bread and wine, show how the sense of taste associated with this chakra is used to awaken the higher senses. 'Oh taste and see how gracious the Lord is' is the translation of one of the Psalms.

The two lower chakras are concerned with the lower part of the body, the feet, the legs and general mobility. Disabilities and restrictions in the hips, the knees, the ankles, or the feet, all indicate a lesson undertaken by the soul to teach patience and give an opportunity to find a freedom of spirit which can rise above physical pain or disability; also to discover the peace of spirit and healing which true forgiveness brings.

While Saturn, planet of limitation and contraction, draws the soul down to earth with the divine fire firmly locked in the base chakra, and ensures that only by steady character-training and self-discipline can it be released, Jupiter, planet of growth and expansion, gives the soul the strong urge and longing to escape, grow wings and fly into the heavens. Both Jupiter and his polar opposite Mercury are portrayed in myth and legend either with wings, or riding on a winged beast, which is symbolic of the power of creative thought and imagination to mould etheric matter according to the heart's desire. Both Jupiter's signs of Pisces and Sagittarius give a deeply religious and devotional side to the nature, and with these signs ruling the hips, thighs and feet, perhaps it is not surprising that through the ages ritual movement and dancing have played an important part in religious ceremonies of many faiths, especially among the races which live close to nature and the etheric world. Their priests and wise men are well aware of the effect of rhythm and movement, and of chanting (Mercury rules the speech organs), in awakening an awareness of this inner world.

This same stimulation of awareness of the inner worlds

comes to those who, with all their heart, sing hymns in a religious service. Music and rhythm play an important part in releasing the expansive jupiterian part of our being (the higher mind) from the rigid earthiness of the saturnian part, with its sense of duty and discipline, and its limiting practicality. It helps us for a brief time to grow wings and rise in spirit into a higher consciousness. The beat or rhythm of pop music and its slightly monotonous chanting has the same effect of releasing psychic energy, but without the direction of the will. When this release is increased with the help of drugs and alcohol, the door to a rather terrifying inner world can be opened, a door not easy to close.

It is interesting also that while Saturn is associated with the mineral kingdom—rocks and stones, metals and crystals—as well as with the practical tasks of mining and shaping these for use, Jupiter in a general way rules vegetation and plant life, with its periods of vigorous growth, flowering, fruiting and decay. He awakens an awareness of the etheric world of fairies, gnomes, sylphs and other elementals, which interpenetrate the nature kingdoms, as well as with the etheric and the subtler bodies of human beings. When either Pisces or Sagittarius is emphasized in a birth-chart there will nearly always be a quickened awareness of the etheric plane and the inner world of nature which brings flashes of foreknowledge, second sight or prophetic dreams.

As the etheric body extends beyond the confines of the physical it seems significant that Jupiter rather than Saturn rules the feet. Saturn governs the knees (Capricorn) and the ankles (Aquarius) but the feet come under Pisces, through which we contact that great tossing sea of etheric substance which is part of the subconscious or submerged self, that sea of etheric memories which holds the story of our past thoughts and actions. Students of reflexology know that the health of the whole physical body is reflected in, and can be treated through, the feet, which are themselves psychic centres, as are the hands. Mercury, the polar opposite of Jupiter, rules the hands, through which psychometrists contact the 'sea of etheric impressions' and healers can channel the stream of renewing life-force to the patient.

White Eagle has often emphasized the significance of the feet and how the physical 'under-standings', when properly used, can help the development of the spiritual understanding. Learning to use them properly, to balance the body weight evenly on them, to stretch and spread the toes, is one of the first steps in the training of *hatha* yoga, that ancient Indian science which recognizes the body as the temple of the soul, each part signifying some spiritual quality which can be developed and trained until the whole being manifests the harmony of spiritual law and lives in unity with God and the universe—a state which leads to perfect health and longevity. In this connection it is interesting that one of the most significant bones in the foot is called the navicular bone—situated in the arch of the foot. Through it we can harmoniously balance and 'navigate' the ship of the body (both the outer and the inner bodies) through the stormy seas of life.

Jupiter and Mercury are planets of travel and exploration, both of places and ideas. Between them they rule all forms of communication, including the publication of books and newspapers; the transmission of news and information by any electronic means, and also all forms of mental training in school, college and university. In the body they are concerned with the blood circulation, the lymph glands, the nervous system, breathing and digestion—all ways in which nourishment and life-force are circulated and distributed, and waste matter eliminated.

The Sun passes through Cancer, the cardinal water sign,

between 21st June and 23rd July in the solar zodiac, and 11th July and 8th August in the lunar. Souls born while the Sun is in Cancer have a special love of home and family, with soul lessons to be learned in this connection. Cancer also gives a love of all growing things and a desire to care for and nurture children, animals, plants and souls needing help. In the early stages of soul growth, this urge to nurture and protect may give a strong sense of the family unit, to the exclusion of outsiders, or an almost overwhelming possessiveness with children, friends or partners. That Jupiter, planet of expansion and growth, is exalted in Cancer, shows how—with gradual development towards selflessness—this possessiveness dissolves and the heart opens in caring sympathy for all living things. The family concept broadens into ever-widening groups, and as this happens there slowly comes true understanding of universal brotherhood. This awareness of the great ocean of divine love is symbolized by the exaltation of Venus in Jupiter's sign of Pisces.

The Sun passes through Scorpio, the fixed water sign, between 24th October and 22nd November. Scorpio is the negative water sign ruled by Mars. It is associated with the eighth house of the horoscope. Here the Moon has its fall (in contrast with its exaltation in Taurus, the builder). Scorpio and the eighth house are concerned with death, or the withdrawal of the life-energy and consciousness into the inner world. Death of the body, and all the legal matters associated with death, come under this influence, which usually stimulates an interest in probing the mysteries of life after death and of the inner etheric world. Scorpio is the sign of secret, hidden matters, and the martian energy focused through this sign and house will quicken the desire to uncover the truth of any condition or situation which needs serious clarification, or seems in any way mysterious. It is helpful for all kinds of research or detective activity and gives much curiosity and desire to experiment.

The crab and fishes are the aquatic symbols of the water signs, but the scorpion, with its deadly sting, lives on the earth and (like the alligator) gives an indication of the danger of unwisely forcing open this chakra, using such devices as ouija boards, or any special practices or exercises designed to stimulate psychic powers before the soul has developed the discrimination and strength needed to deal with the energies that are unleashed. This unfoldment should come naturally through human experience and steadfast aspiration to the higher worlds. The beauty of an insight into the higher worlds, which can come through prayer and religious experience, combined with loving service to others, is sustaining and inspiring, and deeply comforting too, if comfort is needed. This is symbolized by the White Eagle—the higher aspect of the scorpion and the snake (or plumed serpent)—flying towards the Sun.

Physical death, particularly the death of those with whom we have close emotional ties (whether they seem to be positive or negative ones) inevitably stirs our deepest feelings and hidden thoughts. It is not surprising therefore that souls born with this fixed water sign prominent in their birth-charts experience intense emotional reactions, both of love and hate, and they often have lessons to learn through the death of loved ones, sometimes quite early in life.

Many people seem a little afraid or ashamed of admitting to a Scorpio emphasis in their horoscope. They may have a mistaken image of it as 'one of the bad signs'. It is certainly a powerful sign, for the energy of Mars intensifies the emotional nature—but at the same time it gives great self-control. It is never easy to assess what the Scorpio soul is thinking or feeling. A quiet, apparently peaceful exterior can hide a raging torrent of anger, frustration and resentment, which may later manifest in bitter sarcasm or ruthlessly unkind action. At the human level, souls with Scorpio emphasized can acquire an immediate and sometimes quite intense like or dislike for people or conditions. They are in no way logical in this, and it is difficult, especially for the reasonable and dispassionate air signs, to understand the spontaneous emotional reactions of Scorpios. It is useless to argue or try to make them see a logical viewpoint. This merely irritates and makes them more 'set' in their antagonism or devotion to a particular person or cause. But while they will not appreciate reason and logic, they respond to love and affection as flowers to the sunlight, for concealed beneath the Scorpio exterior lies a wonderful warmth of affection, devotion and loyalty.

In the early stages of development, this devotion will be given only to family, or a few friends and co-workers, and much of the emotional energy is devoted to selfish ends. But once the soul has awakened to the light, and the martian energy is directed to wider, more altruistic ends, the devotion, self-sacrifice and true spiritual vision of these souls makes them heroic warriors for the light and among the spiritual leaders of the human race. This sign is prominent in the horoscope of many spiritual teachers, healers, and social workers, and pioneers in medical or scientific research or social reform.

The sacral chakra is linked with the organs of physical generation, but it is equally concerned with the power of creative thought. All the time, by our thoughts and feelings, hopes and fears, we are creating around ourselves conditions which are either harmonious or inharmonious. In fact, negative thought can sometimes be strong enough to create elemental creatures which become attached to the soul, sometimes through several incarnations, and manifest in physical dis-ease. In time, every soul has to learn how to control thought and imagination, using it to create the conditions, both physically and in the soul world, which are truly harmonious for themselves and others.

When the water element is emphasized in the chart, the feelings, emotions and psychic perceptions are particularly active, and when stimulated by inharmonious planetary aspects, can be easily stirred up into great storms of emotion, fear, anger, resentment, self-pity, or depression. These are all tests to call forth the inner creative power which everyone possesses, the power of the Christ within, to still the storm: for the essential lesson of the water element is to find the secret of inner peace and tranquillity.

Souls who are being tested for the water initiation are constantly being given opportunities to let go of petty hurts and over-sensitivity, by making such a clear, strong contact with the Sun in the heart that as it shines on the turbulent waters they become peaceful and still, reflecting the beautiful colour and radiance of the Christ within.

Mars, ruler of the watery Scorpio and the eighth house of death and dissolution of form, is also the ruler of the fiery Aries, the exaltation sign of the Sun. He is the warrior planet, the warrior for the light. Surely the symbolism here is that the fiery energy and will-power of Mars, when wisely directed, will enable the soul to use the Christ power—the Sun-child in the heart—to dissolve and disperse unwelcome thought-forms, putting in their place positive concepts of harmony, joy and thankfulness, which will make a channel for the light of the Sun. The practice of affirmations, especially just as one is falling asleep, can be most helpful in impressing the subconscious mind with health-bringing creative thought.

The Moon, which is closely associated with this chakra through the water element, represents the feminine or receptive side of human nature. She is connected with the inner world of dreams and sleep, during which the soul is able to absorb into the subconscious mind thoughts or affirmations presented to it—not by the forceful and often harsh will-power of the conscious mind, but rather by a gentle, persistent infiltration through quiet affirmations given as the body and mind relax into a state of passivity before falling asleep.

In the helpful book SURYA NAMASKARS: AN ANCIENT INDIAN EXERCISE, by Apa Pant, the yogic author enlarges on this. Preparation for bed at night, he says, should begin with the usual ablutions including evacuation of the bowels and emptying of the bladder. Then, 'As you lie in bed let your mind "massage" all parts of your body from the tip of your toes to the roots of your hair. In a relaxed, quiet state, let your mind rest at the centre of your heart. If you practise a mantra, Name of God, slowly, very faintly, as faint as possible, without moving your lips, let the Name, the sound, which should be as soundless as possible, pervade, invade, cover, all parts of your body as a protecting light, a garment. In this condition of peace, of joy, of Harmony fall asleep. Fall asleep without a care. Give up all cares to God. It is His burden, not yours.

'If you practise falling asleep like this, in the state of dreams, or, in the dreamless state, you will carry on the Yoga of uniting yourself with the totality of Existence....

'In the state of deep sleep, free of the ego-consciousness, the beauty, the serenity, the energy of Life Eternal is available to you. In deep sleep you can become aware of the reality of the unity of Life and thus the truth of Death.

'It is necessary therefore to learn the science of sleep— one-third of your total life.'

The whispered sound of OM, the eastern name for God, the Great White Spirit—Almighty, All-Loving, All-Wise— can gently release mind and emotions from the tensions and strains of the little self into the peaceful realization of the eternal spirit—into the comforting arms of the divine

Mother. This deep relaxation into the heart of the eternal self heals and restores the soul, a healing which will soon manifest in the body and outer mind, bringing inner peace and steadiness and the ability to cope wisely with each problem that arises.

For some people, it may feel easier to whisper the familiar name of Jesus, the Great Healer, or a teacher who has aroused their true love and devotion—for love recognizes and responds to the God shining through another beloved soul. To transfer all one's thought to the love and wisdom of the Master—or of the Great Spirit—and persistently to return to this when the fear and worry thoughts again intrude, will gradually quieten the whole being, especially if the whispered sound is linked with peaceful breathing.

Let the body lie relaxed and comfortable on the hardest, flattest bed available, and follow your own relaxation routine, letting the breath flow gently and easily. Attune yourself to its peaceful rhythm, then turn your thoughts to the Great White Spirit. On each exhalation softly whisper the holy name—imagine the light of the pole star of your own innermost spirit shining down enfolding you in a wigwam of pure white light, and feel the enfolding love of the divine Mother comforting, healing and protecting you, strengthening the Christ light in your heart. Between each whispering of the holy name, gently affirm, '*The Christ light shines in my heart, healing and renewing every cell of my being*', then back into the awareness of the divine Mother's comfort and protection, shining through the feminine aspect of your being as you whisper again the divine name. Gently persist, until sleep overtakes you.

This beautiful healing and renewal which we can train ourselves to receive during sleep, is symbolized in the Babylonian legend of the fish god Oannes who had a man's head on a fish's body. Each day he came from the sea, and taught the savages of that time the rudiments of civilization. At night he returned to the depths of the ocean, to be recharged with the wisdom and love of the Almighty Spirit.

In spiritual healing, when, after an illness or some period of strain the patient seems depleted, White Eagle teaches us to treat the sacral centre through the spleen, which is associated with it. This is in line with C. W. Leadbeater's statements in THE CHAKRAS:

'The spleen chakra is not indicated in the Indian books; its place is taken by a centre called the *Svadhisthana*, situated in the neighbourhood of the generative organs, to which the same six petals are assigned. From our point of view the arousing of such a centre would be regarded as a misfortune, as there are serious dangers connected with it. In the Egyptian scheme of development elaborate precautions were taken to prevent any such awakening.'

And:

'The hypogastric or pelvic plexuses are no doubt connected in some way with the *Svadhisthana* chakra situated near the generative organs, which is mentioned in Indian books but not used in our scheme of development. The plexuses grouped together in this region are probably largely subordinate to the solar plexus in all matters of conscious activity, as both they and the splenic plexus are connected very closely with it by numerous nerves.'

We treat the spleen centre in order to stimulate and energize the circulation of the life-force in the etheric body. White Eagle teaches us to seal this centre after a period of deep meditation, so that we are firmly locked back into the physical consciousness. It is interesting that the seal which he has taught us to use (with all the will and concentration of our spirit), is the equal-sided cross of light encircled by light, a symbol which can also be associated with the four petals in the mandala of the root chakra. Therein lies the *kundalini* fire guarded by the great teacher, tester, disciplinarian and perfectionist, Saturn. While the Jupiter aspect of our nature gives the urge to escape from trials and responsibilities into the freedom of travel, adventure and excitement, either on the physical plane (he rules dancing and acting, and all forms of sport), the mental plane (philosophy) or the etheric plane (dabbling with psychic phenomena or seeking freedom in drugs or alcohol), the Saturn part strengthens our sense of duty and responsibility and points out the path, the narrow hard path up the mountain, which leads to real, rather than illusory, freedom.

All sailors learn early to respect the power and subtlety of the sea, the sand, the rocks and the tides. Similarly, those who would travel on the inner planes must learn to understand the subtleties and dangers, the rocks and quicksands, of that great sea of etheric matter which we enter when the psychic centres are opened. Wise teachers and priests of all religions stress the need for an experienced guide on the path of spiritual unfoldment.

That White Eagle and the shining company in the world of light watch lovingly and in a powerfully protective way over all the souls who in simple faith try to follow his teachings has been proved over and over again through more than fifty years. All souls have lessons to learn, through life's experiences, but are all enfolded in the love of the Brothers in Spirit and always guided safely back on to their own true forward path.

9

THE SOLAR PLEXUS CENTRE
(*MANIPURAKA* AND *SURYA* CHAKRAS)
AND THE FIRE ELEMENT

Soul Lesson: Love, both human and divine
Element: Fire
Sense: Sight
Lotus symbol: Ten petals

THE *MANIPURAKA* centre comes under the fire element, and according to the traditional planetary order has special association with Mars, the ruler of Aries, the cardinal or active manifestation of this element. In Indian philosophy the ram (Aries) is the animal linked with this chakra, which seems to confirm the astrological associations.

The second, or fixed sign of the fire element is Leo, the royal sign, ruled by the Sun. It is interesting that just as Jupiter, the ruler of Pisces and the chief planet of the sacral centre, is exalted in the Moon's sign of Cancer, the Sun, ruler of Leo, is exalted in Aries, indicating the tremendous solar energy which can be released in the *manipuraka* centre, as the desire nature and the astral body are brought under the control of the innermost spirit.

In LIGHT ON PRANAYAMA, B. K. S. Iyengar separates the *surya* (Sun) chakra from the *manipuraka,* the latter residing in the navel, the former above the navel and below the diaphragm. But astrologically, since the Sun is exalted in the Mars sign of Aries, the solar plexus or Sun centre and the Mars centre, the *manipuraka*, are closely linked and we will consider them together as the solar plexus centre.

The third fire sign is Sagittarius, ruled by Jupiter, so we may see that the fire signs of the solar plexus centre are ruled by the same planets, Mars and Jupiter, as are the water signs of the sacral centre, except that here the Sun takes the place of the Moon. The combination of the energies both of the Sun and the Moon in these lower centres, is reflected in the yogic teachings concerning the masculine and feminine energies which exist in every soul—energies which have to be balanced, harmonized, and sublimated to the higher controller as they are drawn up the spine to bring life and light to the subtle bodies. The elements of fire and water working together in the triangle of the lower chakras can together produce a tremendous head of steam, a driving power of sometimes conflicting desires which the soul has to learn to channel, learning the lessons of peace and tranquillity and selfless love.

The solar plexus is the power or energy-centre in the physical body. It is linked with the growth and development of the astral body, and is the seat of intense desire, enthusiasm, action and ambition. Like the sacral centre it can be creative on every plane. All the normal joys and sorrows, the fears and anxieties of our everyday personal life are focused here. Through the fiery emotions of this chakra the soul can be driven on in a certain direction, consumed with desire. It may be the desire for success and achievement, for public acclaim, a longing for emotional satisfaction, for partnership with a certain person, for children and their success, for personal possessions, or more subtly it may be a desire for spiritual attainment, which is perhaps the most tricky of all desires, for it is so subtle and can lead to spiritual pride and consequent downfall of the soul. In fact, the satisfaction of any of the desires can lead to complacency, pride and self-satisfaction.

Also, one desire leads to another, and as soon as one is satisfied the soul drives on to something else. It is always seeking, always wanting; even when the wants are supplied, the restlessness continues.

The astral body, centred in the solar plexus, can thus be a veritable battleground of conflicting feelings. In the earlier stages of development, the soul, placing its consciousness in the astral body, actually revels in a constant succession of different and intense emotional states which can produce lurid colours in the aura. Yet when a degree of mental and emotional control has been attained, the aura will reflect the most beautiful colours of the heavenly consciousness. Thus the solar plexus may be likened to a mirror: a mirror which can reflect either the glory of the Sun in the heavens or the lurid fires of the lower astral regions. It is associated with the sense of sight, and when stimulated will open the vision on the particular plane of consciousness to which the soul is attuned.

The Sun passes through his own sign of Leo from 23rd July to 23rd August (using the solar zodiac) or 8th August and 5th September (using the lunar zodiac). This sign shows the fire element in its fixed mode, steady, powerful, loving and aspiring. Through the fire element, and especially through this the Sun's sign of Leo, the soul gradually learns the lesson of love; learns to distinguish between emotional impulse, which quickens the desire nature, and true love, which is ultimately a complete giving of self, a surrender of the desires and wishes of the lesser self in union with a loved one; or—on a broader basis—an unlimited radiation of warmth and goodwill, an upholding strength which emanates from the soul, almost like the physical Sun, bringing light and life and inspiration to those around.

The fire signs eventually lead the soul to some form of conscious sacrifice, even heroism. Selfish desire is then forgotten in the love of another soul or for some cause to which the heart is given. The solar plexus is the centre of the astral desire body, so when the fire element is emphasized there will always be enthusiasm, aspiration, warmth and impulsiveness in the nature, a fiery driving force which leads to action, wise or foolish, according to how the soul responds to the discipline of Saturn. It is notable that Mars, so closely linked with the solar energy and the *surya* or Sun centre, is exalted in Capricorn, the earth sign ruled by Saturn, a symbol of how the divine energy of the Sun is drawn down into the earth, locked into the root centre, and has to be gradually channelled upwards that it may vivify and illumine each one of the chakras (or psychic centres) until they are all vibrating in harmony and radiating their own specialized energy into the whole being.

Progressively, all the chakras from the base of the spine right up through the body to the head centre blaze with tremendous solar energy, which is directed and controlled by the master in the heart centre. In legend, the Sun god Apollo drives his chariot with seven horses right across the sky: in this symbolism, the life of the physical body is the 'day of life', which is lived in full awareness of the eternal glory of the Sun shining through to beautify every aspect of the life on earth. A similar picture is given in the Bhagavad Gita, in which Krishna (the Lord, the Christ being) is the charioteer for Arjuna, the warrior prince (that is, the illumined personal self). In western symbolism, the Sun drives the chariot of the warrior Mars.

The soul of one who has learned to take the reins of all the planetary forces in his or her own being, radiates an aura of most beautiful colour and fragrance. It is as if all the colours in the aura are singing together, sounding a harmonious note which is the individual ray of that soul, contributing a unique gift to the whole of life.

When the Sun in a fire sign in the horoscope is emphasized by a powerful Mars aspect, the karma could bring opportunities for pioneering work, needing great courage and strength of will. This strength may have been earned by a life of dedication and self-sacrifice in preparation for such a mission. On the other hand, if the martian vibration is checked or hardened by a powerful Saturn aspect, then the soul may meet sorrow and frustration in the present life through older people or perhaps through severe financial restriction, or through a debilitating health condition.

Sometimes in such cases the fiery energy of enthusiasm and desire for achievement can manifest in anger, which, when repressed and turned inwards, can be responsible for severe depression. There is a close connection between the fiery solar plexus centre and the frontal mind, both being associated with Mars. It is natural for the desire nature within us to fight for its own way and to rebel against the restrictions of our karma—but the surrender of self-will into an acceptance of the divine plan in our lives is part of the soul lesson of love.

This acceptance of divine will usually comes when, after some experience of suffering and heartbreak, there is born in a mysterious way a growing faith in the divine love and wisdom which enfolds every life. The true power of the Christ Sun deep in the heart can only begin to shine forth when the desires and ambitions of the personal self have been to some extent outgrown, or until a denial of some dear desire has brought the soul to a point of crucifixion. In myths and stories within every religion, the Sun–Hero sacrifices his life for the sake of a person or a cause. This sacrifice, or rededication of the solar energy, leads the soul to seek the true light, which is to be found in the heart centre. The major tests on the path of initiation are all concerned with the ability to discriminate between the true love and wisdom of the gentle Christ self in the heart and the powerful force of self-will, that solar energy as yet not fully harnessed. The will to accomplish some dear personal desire can so easily over-ride that quiet inner voice of conscience which leads to true illumination, and spiritual unfoldment.

Remembering how the Moon, which represents the limited personality of the present day of life, responds so strongly to the gravity of the earth, it is easy to understand how the solar energy, through Mars, can be focused downwards and become so completely submerged in the concerns of the little self and its personal interests that the soul can almost be classed as dead—dead to the higher spheres of light. Yet when the soul begins to respond to the pull of the Sun its aspiration heavenwards will increase, giving selfless service first to family members and friends whom the soul loves and later to humanity as a whole, in an ever-widening circle of influence.

The solar plexus is the battleground for these two opposing forces, the Moon giving the pull to self-interest and earthly concerns and the Sun giving aspiration towards the higher consciousness, like a flame reaching upwards.

The Sun passes through the cardinal fire sign Aries between 20th March and 19th April. Souls born under the Sun-sign Aries will respond strongly to Mars, this warrior planet of fire, energy and action, which brings to the character strength, self-confidence, courage and independence. He gives the ability to overcome all obstacles through hard work and tenacity of purpose. Ruling the metal iron, he brings to the nature the iron hardness which can bravely endure harsh conditions, but which, unless controlled, can give some harshness or sharpness in dealing with others, a failure to appreciate their sensibilities.

Symbolic of the warrior in battle, Mars rules all weapons of attack, including firearms and articles which are sharp, pointed or hot—scissors, needles, knives and swords—and also irons, furnaces and forges in which iron is tempered into steel. In nature Mars rules plants which are hot and stimulating, such as mustard, pepper, ginger, radish and horse-radish, cactus, gentian, garlic, onion, hops, thistles, briars and nettles, as well as trees which are thorny or prickly. Mars is the planet of vigorous practical action with the will to achieve immediate results. Impetuosity and a hot, fiery temper are weaknesses which may cause him to defeat his own ends by rushing into action without due thought; but courage, energy and endurance enable him to win through seemingly impossible odds to victory.

Martian souls are drawn to work which needs a combination of mental and physical energy, such as engineering, carpentry, surgery, or indeed any activities using sharp, hot, or pointed tools. They will often work in a state of tension and unconscious excitement, anxious to get finished and on to the next job. This constant tension may well make them subject to headaches, migraines, neuralgia, or fevers, as well as accidents and troubles caused by nervous strain.

With Scorpio the tension may be hidden behind a calm manner, but the strain tends to be more emotional than physical or mental, and can cause congestion or inflammation in the excretory or genital organs.

An important lesson for souls on the martian ray is a wise control and direction of the solar energy which flows so strongly through them. They will never be lazy, and always so much feel the need to be 'doing' something that they find real relaxation extremely difficult.

It is interesting that Mars is exalted in the earthy Capricorn, showing how the soul must learn to channel its energy in wise service to the community, with patient persistence rather than with an anxiety for quick results. The slow, steady saturnian vibration will help them to keep on quietly and well, planning and wisely pacing their efforts.

The practice of *hatha* yoga, judo or other martial arts, which teach how to co-ordinate the energies of body and mind, are particularly helpful, as is learning to be aware of unnecessary tension which wastes energy. How many of us, when unscrewing a bottle-top, or performing some simple action, also screw up our facial muscles and clench our teeth! White Eagle has told us often that a Master never wastes energy. We all need to develop our powers of peaceful focus and attention, both in physical and mental activities.

The position and aspects of Mars in the horoscope show how the solar energy, the life-force, is expressed, and whether it manifests chiefly on the physical, mental or emotional plane. Mars is the bringer both of joy and sorrow (which are two sides of the same coin). There is the joy of striving for and achieving some cherished ambition, the joy of effort and pioneering, especially when the energy and enthusiasm are dedicated to the service of some beloved cause or person. Sorrow comes to the martian subject through quarrels and misunderstandings due to a fiery temper or over-impulsive action—and, of course, at the loss of loved ones through death. Since Mars intensifies the desire nature, both joy and sorrow are most deeply felt.

Mars is the essential ruler of the first house of the horoscope, which is linked with Aries, and this house represents the sunrise of the new incarnation, showing the tools with which the pilgrim soul has returned to earth to struggle once more with the problems and trials of physical life and to learn more of the soul lesson indicated by the position of the Sun. The sign of the zodiac rising over the cusp of the first house shows the characteristics of the outer self known to our companions. It gives the physical form and characteristics through which the eternal self—the Christ self—is seeking to fulfil the purpose of the incarnation.

The third of the fire signs associated with the solar

plexus chakra is Sagittarius, the mutable fire sign ruled by Jupiter, through which the Sun passes between 22nd November and 22nd December. Its symbol, the archer with arrow pointing heavenward, clearly indicates the aspiration and ambition of its subjects. 'The sky's the limit' is a good Sagittarian axiom, for Jupiter is traditionally the lord of the sky, with its changing moods and in all its aspects, including thunder and lightning. In Sagittarius the need for freedom manifests as love of travel, by sea or air, and a desire for outdoor activities which provide release of tension for the sometimes over-strained nervous system. The career may well be connected in some way with shipping, travel, or affairs overseas. They may become deeply involved with some kind of sport—especially racing, either with horses, cars or boats, for they love that sense of joyous power which comes with speed. But especially as they grow older, Sagittarians need to be active even more in their minds than in their bodies. The cultivation of the higher mind is important to them; and they are natural students of law, philosophy, religion, medicine, science, spiritual science and metaphysics.

An ancient mystery symbol of Sagittarius was the centaur, a creature with a man's head on the body of a horse. These legendary beings were revered as wise teachers and advisers of gods and heroes, since through their dual make-up they well understood both the animal and divine aspects of human nature. They could help their pupils to discover the source of divine wisdom within their own being, which would give them strength and courage for their labours. This symbol is linked with the positive fiery side of the jupiterian influence.

The two symbolic creatures, Oannes, the fish god, and the centaur, the man-horse, show how Jupiter is concerned with the human mind and consciousness in all its manifestations, from the deepest preconscious—the depths of the ocean—to the subconscious, up to the conscious and finally to that superconscious self which we can only touch in prayer, meditation and during sleep. Through this we can receive wisdom and inspiration from the heaven world through our own guide and teacher. From spirit, Arthur Conan Doyle says:

'Disease originates, not as may be thought in the mental state of the patient, but usually far deeper. It may some-times begin in man's conscious mind it is true, sometimes in the subconscious, but more often in the preconscious. By the last term we mean the condition of consciousness far older than the life now being lived, but one which can be brought over from the man's past lives; a consciousness which extends back through many "ages" or incarnations.'

The upward-pointing arrow of the fiery Sagittarius reminds us of the need within every soul to seek divine inspiration, which can change and illumine the earthly consciousness. It is the instinctive aspiration towards the heavens—almost a reaching for the stars—given by Sag-ittarius that helps the soul to rise out of the purely personal and selfish desire nature to seek spiritual knowledge and understanding.

Sagittarius also reminds us of the other chakras of the lower triangle. In the physical body, while Pisces rules the feet, Sagittarius rules the thighs, hips and sacrum. Both signs are connected with the spleen and the liver, the storehouse of the body's energy, and both are concerned with the flow of the life-force round the body through the bloodstream, the lymphatic and nervous system, and—above all—with the revitalization of the body through the conscious absorption of the divine Breath. Sagittarius and its polar opposite Gemini are closely linked with the magical, vitalizing power of proper breathing.

Few people are aware of the healing strength which can be drawn up through the feet from mother earth. The feet are particularly sensitive and receptive to the life-force, and when we learn to use them properly, to become fully aware of their importance for the health of body and mind, we shall be able consciously to draw upon the strength and wisdom of the divine Mother.

Many modern shoes, especially the more fashionable ones, constrict the toes and throw the whole body out of alignment, so that it is impossible to draw from the earth the vitality available. It is good, whenever possible, to walk about the house with bare feet or clad in warm socks which are loose enough to leave the toes quite free. Practise spreading the toes on the ground, trying to feel each one separately making its individual contact with the ground and drawing into the body its own particular ray of strength and magnetic power.

Jupiter, ruler of Sagittarius, and his polar opposite Mercury, are both linked with hands and feet. The five toes and fingers should be a reminder, not only of the five great laws which govern human life, but also of the five *yamas* and five *niyamas* of yoga which, like the ten command-ments, set out the universal moral precepts which guide us to health, harmony and unity with all life, both on earth and in the heavens. Jupiter is the great law-giver and through the higher mind can generate thoughts and actions which lead to the healthy growth and development of our own Tree of Life.

On the physical plane, the conscious control of posture can greatly help our attunement both to the higher world of light—the Heavenly Father—and to the strength and wisdom of mother earth, the giver of form. With the toes spread on the ground, as described above, and the weight exactly balanced between heels and toes (remember the navicular bone!), feel a gentle pull upwards of the inner body of light, right from the insteps, up the legs and thighs to the heart, and then up to the Star of the higher self, shining above the crown of the head. Gently stretch the back of the neck and relax the shoulders down, away from the ears. Feel as if the feet are sending down roots and drawing the life-force, like the sap of a tree, from the earth and up through the legs and the thighs, steady and firm, right up to the heart which is lifted up and opening towards the heavens. With quiet breathing, feel the light pouring down through the top of the head into the heart where the power and will of the Heavenly Father meet the creative strength of the divine Mother which has been drawn up through the feet. As F. M. Alexander would say, 'Let the inner gaze be deep in the heart' where the two unite—and the light shines forth. This light—the Christ Star—is the master, the healer, the controller of the whole life.

It is helpful to practise 'Tree of Light' breathing* night and morning; for it will strengthen the contact with the divine self and increase the understanding of how the body is the temple of the spirit.

While practising the physical movements of the Tree of Light, it can be helpful to make affirmations from the heart centre. For example, continue with the physical movements and the gentle, rhythmic breathing, until the mind and outer self are quietened and you feel that you are within your own Tree of Light. Feel the beautiful strength of the great tree, the contact with the earth and the heavens, and from your heart make the affirmation: '*My heart is filled with divine peace...divine peace...divine peace*'. Gently repeat this as you become aware that the steady rhythm of your breathing is one with the eternal rhythms of life—of the Sun, the Moon, the tides and the seasons. Feel the light of the Sun glowing within the heart. Then make the affirmation: '*The Christ Sun shines in my heart, permeating*

*See the White Eagle Publishing Trust pamphlet, 'Health and Happiness through the Way you Live'

and healing every cell of my being. Say this, in your heart, three times, quietly breathing in divine strength.

This is an excellent prelude to a few minutes of meditation and quiet breathing, which you can do either standing or sitting, with the spine as upright as possible so that the light can flow up and down the spine. Once you have quietened the outer self with quiet breathing and attunement, you should find two to five minutes of absolute stillness in the heart of the Sun—the Christ self—time enough to give you strength and poise for the day ahead. Then consciously bring yourself back to the outer plane by taking a few deeper breaths and see yourself drawing the light up through the left foot, over the head, and down the right side to complete the circuit, three times, so that you are within a circle of light.

If in this quiet time of realization of the Christ power within, you need help in controlling any special area of your life, just sound the affirmation that the Christ power will help you to achieve whatever specific task lies ahead.

In making such detailed affirmations, it is wise not to give oneself too big a target—take one step at a time in the training and transformation of the lower self, but as White Eagle tells us: 'Keep on keeping on'. If you feel the need to 'put on the whole armour of God' in order to cope with the problems of your outer life, finish the meditation again with one or two sequences of the Tree of Light breathing, drawing the strength of mother earth up through the centre of your being, through your heart, throat and head, stretching your arms gently as high as you easily can above your head. Then bring them down to your side, pausing at shoulder level to form the arms of a cross of light within a circle of light. *Think* this ⊕ as you make the movements.

There is no doubt that every soul can in this way gradually learn to use the beneficent power of the higher mind, the Jupiter energy within, to guide the whole life into ways of peace, harmony and achievement.

Treatment of the solar plexus is one of the vital factors in spiritual healing which can be particularly helpful to the soul worn, weary and confused with the constant struggle. It will help to quieten the stormy emotions and to release any anger, resentment and frustration which blocks the uprising of the Sun-flame. When treating this centre, the healer needs to be deeply peaceful; that is, to open the consciousness to the great angel of peace. As the ray of peace grows stronger, the patient will feel the stormy waves of desire and emotion gradually quietening down until the still water of consciousness reflects the heavens. As Jesus stilled the storm for his disciples and took command of the boat, so the healer can awaken the Christ power, the Sun power, in the patient, so that the energies are directed towards the light. As the higher consciousness begins to awaken, the spiritual guide and teacher of that soul can draw close.

In every life there comes a time when apparent failure or betrayal bring the soul to what seems to be the end of the road: completely defeated, overwhelmed with sorrow and hopeless desolation. As Jesus lay for three days in the grave, closed in by a great stone, so the crucified soul waits in darkness, unaware of the beautiful guardian angel who, enfolding the soul in wings of protection, waits in the silence; but always at the appointed time the angel of the Sun draws close to remove the stone and a new light dawns. No-one is left without help during these darkest hours— the guardian angel is there, pouring light and blessing into the heart until there comes a rebirth, a joyous resurrection.

The exaltation of the Sun in Aries indicates how important is the physical body, and the lessons learnt in earthly incarnation, to the complete development of God-consciousness which will eventually shine through all circumstances of life and give the soul the ability to control the elements, first within his own nature, and then in the world outside. This power has been demonstrated by all the Masters of Wisdom and throughout the ages they have pointed the way to achievement open to every soul.

The Mars element in every one of us is that aspect of our nature which is aspiring, reaching up, first to achievement of selfish ends and then later, after a crucifixion experience, reaching out with renewed strength towards the divine presence. The flame of Star energy within our being, as it aspires heavenwards, unites in the heart chakra with the light of the eternal self and shines forth as a blazing six-pointed Star, the symbol of the soul illumined by the Christ Sun.

10

THE *ANAHATA* (HEART) CHAKRA
AND THE AIR ELEMENT

Soul Lesson: Brotherhood
Element: Air
Sense: Feeling and Touch
Lotus symbol: Twelve petals, at the centre of which
is a six-pointed star

ACCORDING TO their traditional order, the planets associated with the chakras above the diaphragm (the higher
triangle) are Venus and Mercury, whose orbit lies inside
that of the earth with the result that, more so than earth,
they are bathed in the light of the Sun. The Moon, which
as we shall see is linked with the eventual illumination of
the head centres, alternates between the pull of the earth-
magnetism and the full radiance of the Christ Sun; an
astrological feature, but one very easily witnessed with the
naked eye.

The ancient astrologers of Central America made inten-
sive studies of the cycle of the planet Venus, to which they
gave special importance in their worship and ritual. During
her cycle of revolutions round the Sun, there come regular
periods when Venus is invisible from the earthly viewpoint
because her light is lost in the greater light of the Sun, to
which she is so close. After such a period of invisibility, she
appears either rising before the Sun as a morning star, or
setting in the west as the peaceful evening star. For the

Indians of Central America she specially signified the truth of reincarnation. When she appeared as the morning star she was believed to represent all the joy and beauty of youth at the beginning of an incarnation, when life feels eternal and full of opportunities for achievement. When, after another period of invisibility, she reappears as the evening star, she is the warrior bearing the scars of battle, tired or triumphant after the effort of a life spent in service, happy with progress made and sad for the foolish mistakes made during the tests and trials of earth. The soul is ready peacefully to lay down the cares of the physical body and to find rest and refreshment, united with the Sun in the golden world of God. As the morning star she was linked with the immortal heavenly twin Pollux, and as the evening star she would be Castor, the mortal twin, ready to lay down the burden of the body. It is interesting that in the astrology of the ancient Mayans, Venus was not considered to be a feminine goddess, but was linked with the great twin brethren which in our present-day astrology come under Gemini and its ruler Mercury.

The linking of Venus with Castor and Pollux, the great twin brethren of the heavens, seems to be a clear pointer to the magical thirteenth sign of the lunar zodiac, Arachne the spider, which occupies the equivalent of the last five degrees of Taurus and the first twenty-three of Gemini, thus combining the influence both of Venus and of Mercury.

Saturn, the chief planet of the root (*muladhara*) chakra, rules Aquarius and is exalted in Libra, so he also plays an important part in the awakening of the heart chakra. In the ancient Mayan teachings there was, presiding over both Twins, a third god who was regarded as the spirit of the planet as a whole, the one who—as it were—held the scales in which the soul was weighed and tested between each incarnation. In esoteric astrology we could equate this third god with Saturn, who draws the soul back into the bondage of incarnation; who tests, trains and guides our footsteps on the path to mature man–womanhood and to the realization of brotherhood with all life. So here we have the three planets—Venus, Mercury and Saturn—as guardians of the temple of the heart. Identical concepts are depicted in a hieroglyph of the Egyptian Book of the Dead, which pictures the soul after death being weighed in the scales against a feather's weight. This is a symbolic illustration of what happens in the temple of our innermost being when we stand before the flame, the spirit, to review with complete honesty the progress of the life just past and its contribution to the whole panorama of lives through which are gradually building our solar body. This 'day of judgment' comes to every soul at a certain time after death, when all the unwanted material of the lower earthly self is left behind. Rather like a plant in the autumn, discarding dead leaves, flowers and stems, the soul withdraws deep into the root for a period of inner growth, and a review of the next year's development. We are not presented with this 'day of judgment' until we are ready—until within us we have the strength to face the truth, to discover what is wanting to bring the Soul Temple to perfection.

The Sun passes through Arachne between 16th May and 13th June (the dates vary slightly each year). The full Moon that falls in this period is either that of the Buddhist Wesak Festival or the one which White Eagle calls the Christ Moon (otherwise, the full Moons in Taurus and Gemini respectively). Each of these full Moons brings an important opportunity for souls on the path of spiritual unfoldment to open themselves to a special outpouring of light and blessing from the heaven world. They are receptive to this as a result of the quickening of their etheric bodies and psychic centres which occurs as the Sun passes through this sign. Arachne comes under the element ether.

These latter degrees of Taurus and the first twenty-three degrees of Gemini bring into prominence the planets Venus and Mercury, which quicken the higher mental and celestial bodies, enabling us to build a bridge of light between heaven and earth—a bridge of light from the heart of the Sun right down into physical matter.

There is a close link between the heart (*anahata*) and root (*muladhara*) chakras, demonstrated by the fact that Venus, Mercury and Saturn rule the signs of both the earth elements and the air elements. This emphasizes the vital importance that life in the physical body has for the soul's growth to maturity. There can be a temptation, when a soul first awakens to spiritual values, to try to escape from practical, earthly responsibilities and normal human relationships into what White Eagle describes as 'a state of nebulous glorification'—thinking that the spiritual life means floating continuously in clouds of sweetness and light: astrologically, being all air and no earth. Yet the true saints are usually very practical people, who understand how closely linked are the physical and the spiritual worlds. Brother Lawrence and his book THE PRACTICE OF THE PRESENCE OF GOD, above all demonstrate how even the most mundane tasks performed for the love of God (or the love of the God shining through the soul of another) can lift the consciousness into the peace and joy of heaven.

The heart centre or *anahata* chakra is, from the point of view of the aspirant, the key to spiritual unfoldment. It is the centre of our soul life, the inner temple where true guidance can be found, giving light and strength for the path of experience chosen by the soul before coming into physical incarnation. This chakra is especially associated with Venus, and Venus rules Libra, the sign of harmony and balance, in which Saturn is exalted. Saturn, in turn, ruler of Aquarius and polar opposite of the royal Leo gives a growing sense of responsibility to brother man, and to life itself. He disciplines the unruly desire nature and brings tests of patience and endurance which indeed weigh the soul in the scales, but also gradually build that immortal and glorious solar body which all souls will one day use.

Mercury, the next sign in the traditional order, is the ruler of Gemini and Virgo—the signs of scribes, record-keepers and librarians—and thus keeps the record, in the heart centre, of the soul's every response to the tests and trials of daily life and how far it has been true to the inner voice of the spirit, which guides it on the path of brother-hood.

The air element is especially associated with the mind, with the unfoldment both of earthly knowledge and heavenly wisdom, the combination of which will bring to the soul an understanding of the eternal laws which govern life. When people are overwhelmed with the problems and sorrows of their personal karma they come to the point where they say, 'Why, why, why?' 'What is the point of this suffering?' 'Surely there can be no God to allow all this?'. When the need for understanding, the longing for light, becomes so strong that spontaneously the soul goes down on its knees, praying for help and guidance, that prayer is *always* answered.

Between the *surya* and the *anahata* chakras is another minor one, the *manas*, which, according to Mr Iyengar, is the seat of feeling, imagination and creativity, which can be awakened into harmonious activity by correct breathing. It is closely linked with the heart, *anahata*, and when these two are brought into action together they bring devotion and the urge to seek inner knowledge, which helps to free the aspirant from sensual pleasures and develop spiritual-ity.

The Sun enters Gemini on 21st May; it passes out of it on 21st June (solar zodiac) or on 13th June and 11th July respectively (lunar zodiac). Gemini is a particularly volatile sign, showing the element air in its mutable (changeable) mode. The symbol of the heavenly twins is particularly apt because souls with this sign prominent in their charts tend to swing from the heights of joy and inspiration to the depths of depression and lassitude. With their highly sensitive and often tense nervous system, Geminians are liable to suffer from nervous exhaustion, especially if they are tied to a routine job which offers little mental stimulation. They need work which gives them constant change and variety—and possibly short journeys, too. They are good communicators and agents.

They can help themselves greatly by the study and practice of correct breathing, for Gemini rules the lungs, shoulders, arms and hands. In the physical body there is a particularly close association between the heart and the lungs, for the venous blood, carrying the impurities absorbed during its circulation round the body, is pumped into the lungs to be cleansed and revitalized. Seekers of true spiritual communion soon realize the importance of the control of breathing, closely affecting the nervous system and the etheric body. The diaphragm, the large umbrella-shaped muscle which divides the lower from the higher triangle of chakras, is an important factor in breath control. Professional speakers and singers understand this, but it is not quite so evident that in spiritual unfoldment this muscle also plays a vital part in developing and strengthening a conscious link with the higher mind, the eternal wisdom in the heart. Learning how to become attuned to one's own quiet breathing rhythm is a vital step, both in meditation and in spiritual healing.

When we consciously quieten the breathing and try to focus the mind on the Christ light in the heart, we begin to absorb into every cell of our being not only the oxygen, the gasses which energize the physical life, but the life-force of God, which builds and strengthens the body of light. The bloodstream becomes filled with light and vitality. As it flows round the body it brings new life and strength to all the cells, cleansing away impurities. But even more than this, the quiet steady breathing helps in the control and direction of thought power, so that the healing light of the spirit can radiate with increasing strength and effectiveness to heal other souls in need. This is the special lesson of the air element which is an important factor in the progress of humanity into the new age of Aquarius.

The heart chakra and the air element quicken the sense of touch or feeling. As the lessons of the elements are gradually absorbed and their special qualities built into the Soul Temple, the heart chakra becomes increasingly active, so that the sense of feeling expands into a wide, loving attunement with all life. We begin to feel really 'in touch' with the world of nature, with our animal friends; with friends and loved ones on earth and in the world of spirit— for in this unfolding consciousness of the brotherhood of all life there can be no separation, no death; only change and growth, with an increasing awareness of the needs of those about us and a loving response to those needs. Most of all, we truly know that we live and move and have our being in God, whose divine love, wisdom and strength 'always has met and always will meet every human need'. We are at peace.

The heart chakra, the base of the higher triangle, is situated in the centre of the thorax, the body cavity formed by the twelve thoracic vertebrae and the twelve pairs of ribs attached to these, which enclose and protect heart and lungs. This chakra, by analogy, is encircled by the twelve signs of the zodiac and the soul lessons which they bring. The mandala of this chakra is the twelve-petalled lotus, at the centre of which is a six-pointed Star. Until the soul has gained sufficient experience through the lower chakras to develop a good, strong grip on the physical life, and an understanding of the practical needs of its fellow men, it is not really ready to start the spiritual search. With worldly interests paramount, there are too many exciting aims and objects to pursue, too many personal desires to be satisfied. This is a necessary stage in soul growth, giving a firm foundation of knowledge and experience through which the quality of discrimination develops. Then, usually after some suffering, bereavement or failure, or even boredom with material pleasures, the soul begins to long for light on the path ahead, and a faith that will sustain it.

White Eagle explains the story of Exodus in terms of the soul's urge to free itself from the entanglements of the lower desires. In the biblical story, Moses led the Israelites (the children of the Sun) out of the land of Egypt, out of the house of bondage, to seek the Promised Land; but this was only a beginning, for the Promised Land was still a long way off, and there were many wanderings in the wilderness and periods of disquiet and grumbling for the Israelites before they found what they sought. This period of training is shown by the circle of the zodiac, with the lessons and tests of the twelve (or thirteen) signs which are understood at a deeper level as the heart chakra begins to open. In THE PATH OF THE SOUL White Eagle gives an interpretation of the soul lesson which every element teaches, the key to esoteric astrology.

Both Venus and Mercury can only manifest their inner and finer qualities when the soul has begun to awaken to spiritual values and—like Christian in Pilgrim's Progress— has consciously made the decision to tread the path which leads to realization of the golden world of God. As the awareness becomes increasingly settled in the awakening heart-mind, bringing an increasing sense of unity and brotherhood with all life, the higher chakras in the throat and the head also begin to quicken. White Eagle teaches that the safe and most harmonious way for all these centres to develop is through the growth of human and divine love in the heart centre.

Saturn, ruler of Aquarius, and closely linked with these two planets in the heart centre, has often been called the 'bridge' to the higher worlds. He strengthens our sense of responsibility until we realize intuitively that it matters not how many spiritual exercises of mind or body we practise, none of them can be really effective until the heart centre, made tender by experience, opens in brotherly love and service to all life. Then the beauty of Venus begins to manifest in the building of a perfect celestial body, while the angel of Mercury spreads his wings in the heart and raises the consciousness into the celestial spheres, awakening the throat centre and finally combining with the planet Uranus, the light-bringer, to give that glorious illumination of consciousness where we know no separation between earth and heaven.

Regularly the bright planet Venus shines in the morning or the evening sky, close to the rising or the setting Sun. In the same way she shines in the clear sky of the inner consciousness, bringing to the soul a longing for peace, harmony and beauty. She has above all a refining influence on our lives. She is the planet of human love and happiness, through which experience there gradually grows in each of us an understanding of divine love. When Venus is harmoniously placed and aspected in a birth-chart, especially with the Moon, she can bring much happiness through family life, friendship and relationships. She gives a spontaneous appreciation of beauty in form, sound and colour, and so is usually prominent in the birth-charts of artists and musicians, sculptors, interior decorators, dress-designers, beauticians and all who work in some way to bring comfort, harmony and beauty into everyday life.

Her cardinal (active) air sign Libra (23rd September—23rd October) is associated with the seventh house of the birth-chart, the house of marriage and partnership of all kinds; or on the other side of the coin, of open enmity and conflict, of law-suits and legal battles or—in national horoscopes—war. Planets in the seventh house can also signify a lifestyle which brings one in some way before the public.

All the air signs teach the soul lesson of brotherhood. The Venus aspect of human nature manifests in our close relationships, either peaceful or otherwise, according to her position and aspects with other planets in the horoscope. She gives the desire to promote harmony, unity and understanding of another's viewpoint, and gives a tactful easy manner, with a natural sense of diplomacy which enables one to steer clear of tricky situations which might lead to a breakdown in negotiations. Souls with Venus strongly placed, or a libran emphasis in their charts, could become skilled mediators, bringing conflict and dissent to a peaceful conclusion.

Physically Libra rules the kidneys and adrenals, and like all the air signs sensitizes the nervous system, which is quickly upset by inharmony in the environment.

Just as Venus through her earth sign Taurus builds on the physical and etheric plane, so through her air sign Libra she helps us to use the power of thought to build into the soul those light atoms which enable it to bring beauty, health and harmony into manifestation in the physical body and the surrounding conditions.

Since Leo rules the physical heart, it seems strange that the heart chakra is linked not with the fire element, but with air; but the Sun, ruler of Leo, is the polar opposite of Saturn, ruler of Aquarius, and the two work together through the heart centre to bring an understanding of the true brotherhood of the spirit, which is the lesson of the Aquarian Age. Saturn, Venus and Mercury are all concerned with the development of the higher mental and celestial bodies, through which the Sun-flame of the eternal self can shine in full radiance; but their function is more subtle than is generally understood. They can only fully manifest their unique qualities as the higher chakras become activated by the divine fire of pure love, with its sacrificial quality, which has developed through the human life-experience of the lower triangle of chakras.

It is easy to understand why White Eagle so often speaks of the mind in the heart as being the source of wise guidance for the soul; but why should Venus and Saturn have such an important part to play in connection with the heart centre, the temple of the eternal spirit where dwells the Sun-flame which guides every soul through its life on earth?

First, let us consider the inner symbolism of Libra, the scales. It represents the eternal law of balance, one of the five great laws which govern human life. It shows the perfect balance which every soul must learn to achieve, between the outer and the inner life, the material and spiritual worlds of being, between the higher and the lower self; and also in all human relationships. It is in the heart that the energies of the higher and lower triangle of chakras have to be balanced to form the perfect six-pointed Star, symbol of the mystical marriage of mind and heart, or the Christing of the human soul.

This harmonization of opposites must come in the heart centre, so Saturn, ruler of Aquarius, the complement of the Sun sign Leo, must eventually balance and direct the powerful solar force as it flows through mind and body. This solar force is channelled through the desire nature of fiery Mars (the polar opposite of Venus), which energizes the solar plexus and sacral centres. It is interesting how these two planets, quickening the chakras on either side of the *surya* chakra—the Sun—work together to transmute fiery desire and passion into selfless love and service. Mars, through Aries, rules the energetic frontal mind—the head mind—which is needed for service in the outer world. Venus rules the mind in the heart, and with pure creative thought builds the sanctuary where the innermost spirit, the eternal flame, burns peacefully. The flame gradually transforms the whole life by reflecting its gentle creative power into the heart-mind, while the angels of Venus which surround the flame radiate it into the outer life.

Saturn, the strict disciplinarian, ensures that every lesson is perfectly learned and every wrong righted before the soul can proceed to the next step. The hardships and frustrations which he brings help to develop the patience and inner strength which prepare us for greater opportunities on the spiritual path, for greater joy and achievement. Saturn's exaltation in Libra again emphasizes the divine law of balance which ensures that however hard the lesson, there is always some compensation—some manifestation of the grace of God in the life.

Difficult karma and suffering force the soul to turn inwards towards the centre of peace, the spiritual Sun in the heart, through which it will come to know the ministrations of the divine comforter. The gentle ray of Venus, planet of heavenly grace and love, will gradually melt away bitterness and resentment until self-pity gives place to true forgiveness and understanding, and an awakening of brotherly love in the heart.

As we have seen, quiet, peaceful breathing helps us to bring into operation this gentle grace, which tranquillizes an overwrought nervous system and calms stormy emotions. In this way we can gradually bring peace and relaxation to the tense, weary body. We consciously let go of troubles, pain and anxiety when we centre our thoughts on the steady rhythm of the breath. Through conscious gentle breathing, we become attuned to our own natural soul rhythm. Thus we can respond increasingly to the influence of the higher world and the angels of Venus, who draw close to enfold us in heavenly peace. We open our hearts to the loving companionship of the shining brethren in the world of light, who strengthen, comfort and support us through our hard, saturnian testings.

When faced with difficult karma, it can be helpful to remember that this is an opportunity to learn how to bring into operation the creative power of Venus, which, through the airy Libra, is concerned with the building power of thought. Through Taurus, the builder, this power is usually manifested on the physical plane—the bricks and mortar that we see all about us. Yet there is a more subtle power, that of Venus, which can build beauty and harmony into the physical life just as strongly, through creative thought. Positive thoughts of kindness, forgiveness, beauty and hopefulness build into the aura those light atoms which enable us to be increasingly responsive to the inspiration and guidance from the Brotherhood of Light in the higher worlds.

It is helpful also to remember that indulging too much in feelings of guilt and shame is a negative exercise, but through the creative thought-power of Venus, planet of heavenly love and thus of forgiveness, we have the opportunity to set right the balance and bring healing where we may have inflicted pain.

The heart is the centre where we learn to harmonize all the conflicting elements in our nature—all conflicts of mind or emotion. This balance between the inner and outer mind, the higher and the lower self, is beautifully symbolized in the six-pointed Star—the star of Venus, whose mystical number is six. Brightly she shines as the morning or evening star—leading us into the sunrise of a new day, or gently drawing us back into the golden world of God.

Modern science and the space programmes appear to

have proved that there is no life, in the sense in which we understand it, on Venus. Nevertheless, we must realize that there are planes of existence that we cannot see or touch with our purely physical senses. Even the lower etheric body, which so closely interpenetrates the physical, is virtually invisible to the majority of people; and the astral body is even less seen, while the higher mental and celestial bodies are beyond the inner vision of any but sages and adepts who understand the secret of contacting these inner worlds. Venus, being so close to the Sun, is connected with the higher mental and celestial plane, and the life lived there is beyond our present comprehension. We are told by White Eagle and other spiritual teachers that life on Venus is far more beautiful than our earthly minds can possibly conceive. She is the planet of true brotherhood, the centre from which, throughout the ages, great teachers have come to the earth to demonstrate divine love in human form and to bring once again to mankind the pure, holy and saving teaching of that ancient and eternal Brotherhood of Light.

Saturn's sign of Aquarius, through which the Sun passes between 21st January and 19th February, teaches the soul lesson of brotherhood. The air signs are all concerned more with the mental than the physical plane, affecting the mind and the nervous system, quickening our response to the inner, higher planes of being. Through his exaltation in Libra, Saturn gradually teaches the soul to hold the balance between the determined wilfulness of the lower self, and the aspiration towards brotherly love and understanding which is the basic principle of Aquarius, his positive sign.

It is in the heart chakra, in the light of the Christ Sun, that the cold, determined practicality of Saturn and the signs it rules gradually changes from self-will and self-seeking to an increasing desire to serve others. Thus the individual discovers a heavenly wisdom which can only come through the heart-mind, the mind of the higher self, as it grows in awareness of the unity of all life and of the brotherhood of men and angels. It is from the heart centre that the soul sets up its 'Jacob's ladder' to the heavenly consciousness, as selfish desire and ambition drop away.

The intellectual reasoning mind and the subconscious body-mind will blend with the loving wisdom of the mind in the heart, which White Eagle calls the superconscious mind, bringing about that mystical marriage described in occult philosophy. Appropriately, Libra is the sign of partnership and marriage.

Saturn can help us to achieve a wise discipline of body and lifestyle which can do much to ensure the comfort and ease of good health; also to control and direct thought-power, creating a channel through which divine magic can strengthen and renew the whole being. This, every soul learns in time.

Aquarius is specially concerned with thought-control, which comes through understanding the life-giving power of the breath. Quiet, controlled breathing opens the heart and the higher mind to the renewing life and strength of the divine self which flows through the bloodstream, restoring and healing every cell.

The power of Saturn is specially felt during the latter years of life—after the age of seventy, when the basic rhythm of nature indicates a gentle surrender of a number of physical responsibilities and a withdrawing from the outer to the inner life. At this time there can be a conscious building of the bridge between the two worlds through mental and physical discipline, which in turn brings into the heart-mind a subtle attunement to the quiet inbreathing and outbreathing of nature. There comes an inward reali-zation of, and harmonization with, the eternal rhythms of life—of the tides and seasons; and the rhythm of the great cycles of eternity. In the heart there comes to the wise soul a feeling of flowing with the tide of life, a peaceful acceptance of winter as a period of rest and withdrawal, but also of inner rebirth and renewal.

Christmas, the celebration of the Capricorn solstice, is a time when we think with joy of the new-born Christ babe, and comes as a lovely symbol for every soul who is suffering the limitations and frustrations of difficult saturnian karma. It brings new hope, and a sure knowledge that out of every form of discipline and human suffering this beautiful Christ-consciousness is being born and strengthened in the heart, bringing a peace beyond all earthly understanding.

11

THE *VISUDDHA* (THROAT)
CHAKRA AND THE ELEMENT ETHER

Soul Lesson: Union
Element: Ether, or space
Sense: Hearing and Listening
Lotus symbol: Sixteen petals round a white open circle

THE ELEMENT associated with the Visuddha chakra is ether, or space, and its symbolic lotus has sixteen petals (four times four). Ether combines the subtle essence of the other four elements, and could be likened to the pinnacle of the Great Pyramid, from which, in past ages, the rays of the sun were reflected in such brilliance that they radiated throughout the land of Egypt. White Eagle gives an inner meaning to this, saying that the land of Egypt can symbolize the physical body.

As the twelve lessons of the elements, represented in the twelve signs of the zodiac, are gradually mastered, the soul begins to develop its own unique quality along the lines of the seven planetary rays, mirrored in the body by the seven cervical vertebrae in the neck, which are linked with the throat centre.

The unfoldment of the throat chakra will lead the soul to a wider and deeper understanding of the eternal, unchanging truths of life. It is linked with the sense of hearing, both on the physical and spiritual plane, and with the vocal cords and the production of sound. The planet traditionally associated with this chakra is Mercury, ruler of Gemini and Virgo. Mercury's polar opposite is Jupiter, ruler of Sagittarius and Pisces, indicating the close relationship between the throat and the spleen chakra. Gemini, Sagittarius and Pisces are all mutable signs, dual in character, signifying the union between the heavenly and earthly consciousness, which all the signs of mutable or *sattvic* (wisdom) quality help to develop. Both Jupiter and Mercury are associated with the nervous system and the etheric body, which is the bridge between the world of spirit and the world of matter, and is itself dual in character. The lower etheric is closely integrated with the physical through both the nervous system and the ductless glands. It continues to function for a short while after the death of the physical, but then is withdrawn and reabsorbed into the ether—the great ocean of life.

The higher etheric body lives on, becoming the vehicle of the arisen soul, the body of light through which the astral, mental and celestial bodies can function. For some time after physical death the soul continues to live on the higher astral plane (the 'Summerland' as described by the Spiritualist), in much the same way as on earth, but freed from the stresses of time, space and economic necessity. Work is joy, because there is every facility for creative enterprise, for learning, for research, for serving and helping others and for expressing any gifts of mind and spirit that have been awaiting an opportunity to develop.

While the soul is imprisoned in the physical body, the higher and lower etheric both merge with the physical atoms, and the lower etheric body extends perhaps an inch or two beyond the physical, where it is sometimes visible as a bluish shadow; while the higher etheric forms an aura visible only to clairvoyants, according to the level of consciousness they can reach.

Gemini is the sign of communication—of thoughts

expressed in sound or symbol; and as the throat centre becomes active the soul begins to feel a longing to communicate—to sound its own individual note in the grand harmony of the universe. Sound has great creative power, and as this chakra unfolds many new spiritual faculties are brought into operation. The quality associated with the throat chakra is purity, on every plane of being. It is linked especially with Virgo, sign of purity, discrimination and childlike humility. Virgo it is who causes the soul to say, *Behold the handmaid of the Lord; be it unto me according to thy word.*

As the throat chakra becomes more active, the mental powers are often strongly emphasized and, as with the sacral and *manipuraka* chakras associated with Jupiter, there can be a danger of mental pride and arrogance, barring the path to true spiritual union with the Divine which the soul seeks. The soul may become like the Israelites wandering in the wilderness of the mind, mistaking the manna in the wilderness (the many different methods of seeking spiritual understanding on the mental plane) for true spiritual food.

The path of simplicity, humility and dedicated service is not easy to find. Its entrance is the narrow gate described by the Master. But when the soul can stoop to enter, the illumination of understanding which comes is deeply satisfying, for it brings an inner peace from which there radiates a wonderful healing power. Virgo, the exaltation sign of Mercury, is associated with health and healing, with diet and medical matters. Many doctors, nurses, dieticians and health workers have this sign or house prominent in their chart.

The throat chakra can become a centre of great power, which will only be fully developed as the soul becomes balanced and proficient in the lessons of the four elements, and as the mind in the heart becomes active. This is a similar process to ordinary education. The student has to pass a general examination in all subjects before he or she can begin to specialize.

The square base of the Great Pyramid gives a clear illustration of the need for a firm, exact foundation in the building of the Soul Temple—a foundation of love, manifesting through self-discipline, humour, tolerance and common sense, which is gradually built through the human experiences brought to us in the lessons of the signs of the zodiac. In the little handbook AT THE FEET OF THE MASTER, which was Krishnamurti's first work, the four essential qualities are described as Discrimination, Desirelessness, Good Conduct and, most important of all, Love.

Without this sure, steady strengthening and character-training, the soul is not ready to progress along the special lines of development of the planetary rays which involve a conscious link with the angelic powers. Such specialized interests may start in a spontaneous way as a hobby which becomes all-absorbing as the fascination grows. Most people will accept much tedious and repetitive work when their hearts are set on the end in view, so that gradually they develop the necessary skill and understanding to become experts along their own lines—whether this be some form of sport or physical activity, art, creative enterprise, scientific investigation or the path of spiritual unfoldment. No matter what line of interest is chosen, there must inevitably be long periods of tedious and often repetitive work and practice in order to achieve a professional standard and become master of a craft. The base of the pyramid has to be four-square—exact, perfect and true.

For the soul who seeks to follow the path of spiritual unfoldment, this is specially the case. There are no short-cuts to the pinnacle of illumination, for as soon as we seek contact with the inner planes of being, we meet constant and increasingly subtle tests which will build in our souls the strength, wisdom and humility needed to cope with the powerful angelic rays which will play upon us in our work and service.

White Eagle says: 'The entrance to the halls of wisdom and initiation can only be granted after the soul has conquered the lower nature. No soul is allowed to crash through the gates of initiation, and you cannot receive initiation by reading books about. But even the simplest, humblest soul on earth can be admitted to the Temple of Initiation—it is the result of selfless and pure love and a truthful sincere life. God bless you with this blessing.'

There is no doubt that the safest form of spiritual development for most students comes through the unfoldment of the heart chakra. Any occult or religious activity which does not first awaken warmth, kindness and a wise understanding of the human need of others, can lead to serious problems; for without this gentle love and willingness to serve, the stimulation of spiritual pride is a real danger. It can lead to power-seeking and the desire to dominate others through the force of a highly developed self-will (amplified by the darker angelic rays)—desires which inevitably result in suffering.

As the heart chakra becomes more radiant and active, the soul will begin to feel a particular leaning towards one of the seven planetary rays (which are fully described in ASTROLOGY THE SACRED SCIENCE). Increasing interest and absorption in a certain line of development will carry the soul forward with greater zest and enthusiasm; and there may come incarnations when a particular planetary ray may manifest so strongly that the soul will show genius in a certain direction and give special service to the world in that particular incarnation, as in the case of great musicians, religious leaders, healers or scientists with a mission of service and inspiration. To quote Dr Johnson, 'The truegenius is a person of large general powers, accidentally determined to some particular direction'.

It is at this stage of spiritual development, when there comes a strong urge to serve humanity, that aspirants are led to some centre or school, such as the White Eagle Lodge, where they can begin to learn to work with the angels of the seven rays on the inner etheric plane. This co-operation with the angels, the brotherhood of angels and men, is developing increasingly as we advance into the Aquarian Age.

At the present time the soul of humanity is being quickened, and many people are being led to some under-standing of the spiritual power and deeper lessons of the signs of the zodiac. Those who have reached this point of desiring to serve are always led to an opportunity to work in some spiritual capacity: for instance, in the context of the White Eagle work, as part of an absent healing group where one learns, in a very simple way, how to become attuned to the angelic powers, using colour rays in co-operation with the angels of healing. This not only gives an oppor-tunity to bring light and healing to souls in need, but it also helps the healer to develop the thought-control which is a vital factor in the projection of the light. Again, the symbol of the Great Pyramid is helpful, for if we think of the mathematical perfection of those triangles and the focus of spiritual power and light at the apex, we can perhaps gain an idea of how exact and perfect the thought-control must become before we can develop the full potential of the throat chakra.

Mercury rules the organs of speech, and souls who are beginning to unfold the power of this centre will often be drawn to speaking, lecturing, teaching, writing, or journal-ism—any work through which thoughts and ideas are conveyed to the public. In Greek symbolism, Mercury was always represented as the young boy, the servant of Jupiter, who had to be well-directed and kept occupied by his master, for otherwise, just out of fun, he could cause immense mischief.

Those who come strongly under Mercury, especially those called to follow a spiritual path, need the help and control of a wise teacher to assist them to develop discrimination and spiritual awareness so that they learn to recognize and obey their own master, the light within. It is simple truth, but not as easy as it sounds; for many times we confuse the true inner light of the spirit with the self-will of the desire nature, the wolf in sheep's clothing which can so easily lead the soul astray through arrogance and self-assertiveness. This is one of the greatest hazards of the rapid mental development of the present age, in which young people are encouraged to 'do their own thing' without being given an understanding of the self-discipline required and the matching need for *every* soul to serve life in some way. There is often an encouragement to selfishness, which only leads to confusion and unhappiness. The path to spiritual illumination is always through the gentle unassuming sacrifice of personal desires in loving service to all life.

At our present stage of evolution, comparatively few souls can fully respond to the finer vibrations of Venus and Mercury. Who can express in words the beauty and peace which can flow from the heart of the spiritual Sun into the higher consciousness, especially through the heart and throat centres, to permeate the whole being of man? Mercury, the messenger of the gods, the planet of divine wisdom and intelligence, rules all forms of communication. One might almost imagine him as the 'divine computer' through which the higher consciousness—when fully developed—can draw upon the total wisdom of the Cosmos. But divine wisdom and love must always have a vehicle of expression, a vehicle which is created by the divine Mother with the help of the angels of Venus (ruler of Taurus and Libra) out of the white ether—the most subtle form of matter. This has to be shaped by conscious thought and will, first on the celestial plane then the higher mental and astral, then on the lower mental, and the various astral planes of the 'Summerland', down through the etheric world of the nature kingdom and into physical manifestation on earth, and through the earth element in human nature. Even Taurus, the steadiest, most stolid, practical and reliable of the twelve signs, has yet a close affinity with the etheric plane and the fairy world of nature, while Virgo brings that purity of heart which enables the soul to see God—everywhere and in everything.

On the spiritual path, souls who are beginning to feel the power of the angels through their service, such as in healing groups and in radiating light to humanity, as well as in a practical everyday way, will be tested many times and in subtle ways for their humility, simplicity and heart's devotion to their spiritual teacher. This is the 'narrow way': one might even liken it to the eye of the needle, through which the soul must pass before it can enter the realization of the Kingdom of Heaven.

With the development of the throat chakra there will gradually come a complete balance, a drawing together of the masculine and feminine qualities in the soul, into that true balance through which the light shines. This is symbolized in Mercury's staff—the magic wand Caduceus, the intertwined snakes depicting the positive and negative life-forces, criss-crossing at certain points (the chakras) as they rise up the spine to bring illumination to the head chakra, *sahasrara*.

The development of the heart chakra awakens and strengthens human love, bringing an ever-growing sense of responsibility for the happiness of others. As the throat chakra develops, this human love broadens to include the angelic kingdom and all life, a recognition of a universal brotherhood, a caring for every aspect of life and nature. Caring also involves the discrimination and discipline shown by a wise gardener who knows how to prune hard; or by the wise spiritual teacher who well understands that the severe tests the aspiring soul meets are necessary in order to make him or her strong enough to stand the tremendous power of the cosmic rays it will encounter when it works with the angelic beings. These are the lessons unfolded by the planets Mercury and Jupiter, as the development of the throat chakra also stimulates the creative power of the jupiterian sacral chakra, which opens the door to the etheric world.

We are only at the very beginning of this path of spiritual knowledge, a science which comes not with the development of the frontal mind and the earthly brain, but with the unfoldment of the higher consciousness. This consciousness comes from the heart and eventually blooms in the crown centre as the thousand-petalled lotus of cosmic consciousness.

12

THE HEAD CENTRES

AJNA: associated with the Sun and Uranus
SOMA: associated with the Moon and Neptune
LALATA: associated with Mercury and Pluto

IN THE PHYSICAL body, the head and face are ruled by Aries, the exaltation sign of the Sun. Astrologers will see in this rulership not only a link between the solar plexus (the fiery astral or desire body) and the frontal brain, but also the symbol of that divine illumination which comes when the solar body is fully developed.

The *ajna*, situated between the eyebrows, is known as the centre of command, or in the words of B. K. S. Iyengar, 'the abode of joy'. The full activation of this chakra brings command over all the cells of the body, through which the soul can experience the joy of divine life on every plane of being.

This centre is associated with the Sun, which is exalted in Aries, the cardinal fire sign, ruling the head and face. The energy and activity of this Mars sign can make the frontal mind a battleground of thoughts and ideas, just as the solar plexus is a battleground of emotions. When the focus of the life's experience is upon the activity of the frontal brain, it is easy to see how the dominance of Mars and Aries stirs up the soul energies so that instead of reflecting divine intelligence and wisdom, the mind entirely reflects intellectual ideas, theories and ideologies. This intellectual aspect of the mind can be extremely separative. The yogi works towards the union of the 'little self' with the eternal self, but when the frontal mind is over-stimulated there tends to be a dominant self-will; the desire for complete independence will overcome the urge of the soul towards union. This is not to say that the need to establish a personal identity is wrong, for the discovery of our true individuality is the purpose of our incarnation in matter. Every soul is indeed unique and, like the prodigal son, has to travel a long road to establish its individuality. The experience of the journey, and the soul's reaction to every experience, completes the building of the perfect individuality in which the soul at last recognizes that only through union with the divine Mind can it find true sonship. Then, in the realization 'I and my Father are one', it manifests the perfection of the Cosmos.

In THE RETURN OF ARTHUR CONAN DOYLE, Sir Arthur says 'I want to emphasize this truth again and again. With the eternal and absolute God there can never be any question of absorption; and yet it is all absorption. Here is a paradox—but do you not see? In becoming *one* you become a part of *all*; in becoming *all* you must become *one* with God. This is a magnificent and transcendent thought. Could man only grasp, if only momentarily or occasionally, some faint glimmer of this truth, world affairs might take a mighty turn for the better. World friction would cease because man would be translating himself from the *personal* point of view to a realization of his true nature. It was to this that Jesus Christ strove to awaken men.

'While we are here we would leave...another thought to mature in your minds. On the plane of consciousness we have called the universal, which means the allness of all life, man can control the elements, and create at will by filling his consciousness with the universal creative life-force. This is the secret of which the Masters make use; by operating in accord with that universal vibration they overcome (or rather control) all the material elements around them. With equal facility they control not only the material but the astral and mental elements in their respective spheres.

'It can be done by a Master who can by an effort of his spiritual will-power (not the will-power of his physical mind) raise and so quicken his vibrations as to attract the atoms of any of these differing planes to himself. When they have accumulated, he gradually lowers or slows them down until they become no longer spiritual but physical atoms, to be formed into whatever article or substance he desires.'

In certain methods of meditation, concentration is focused upon the centre between the eyebrows, known sometimes as the third eye. When fully awakened, this centre gives the seeker conscious command over every cell of the physical body, which radiates the light of the spiritual Sun and brings to the soul a sense of joy and command. In one flash there can come a vision of eternal things—of the glory and majesty of the Creator. White Eagle associates this chakra with the planet Uranus, known in esoteric astrology as the 'lightning flash'.

But unless the soul is ready—tested and strengthened by devotion and discipline of body, mind and emotions—this lightning flash can be unbearable, almost devastating to the physical vehicles. Until the throat centre, the *visuddha* chakra, is well activated, the soul is not usually ready to receive the impact of this divine illumination, which can shatter the whole nervous system, just as a lightning strike can splinter a tree. The wise teacher who understands his pupil's needs and soul capacity is at his most needed at this stage.

Visuddha means purity. The activation of the throat centre gradually raises the quality of simple human love to a divine compassion and understanding, to a wise love which is above all petty hurts and selfish claims—a love which brings a sense of unity and brotherhood with all forms of life. As this love–wisdom grows, and the soul becomes increasingly selfless, the power of understanding widens and the mind becomes at once stronger and more positive, yet simpler and more humble. The soul begins to recognize God everywhere, in even the tiniest manifestation of life. *Blessed are the pure in heart,* says Jesus, *for they shall see God.*

To the soul who has reached a state of childlike simplicity and purity, the lightning flash of illumination which comes with the awakening of the *ajna* chakra can bring nothing but intense joy.

The *visuddha*, or throat chakra, is associated with speech and sound, with the expression of thought and the power of the creative Word. The Word, which is sounded from the throat chakra, can be associated with the Taurus phase of Arachne—Taurus, which is ruled by Venus, and the sign in which the Moon is exalted. The *soma* centre, deep in the centre of the brain, is linked with the Moon. Mr Iyengar tells us that its activation regulates the temperature of the body.

Interpreting this at a more subtle level, it is easy to see how the peaceful calm of the full Moon, shining on the waters of the soul, can balance the fiery heat of the Sun and Mars, which can become much too strong if the *ajna* centre is stimulated too soon.

It is worth remembering that besides the sounding of the creative Word, the *visuddha* and *soma* centres are also concerned with the sense of hearing, and the art of listening. Truly to listen, all the noisy thoughts which jostle for attention must be quietened, and the instrument—the etheric body—must be consciously tuned to that state of quiet listening where the soul becomes aware at a deeper level; aware of the cry for help, hidden perhaps in the angry, bitter words of another; aware of the subtler sounds and harmonies of nature in garden, field and woodland; and most of all, aware of that gentle voice of command, the still small voice of the Master, the Christ within, which is such a sure guide on the spiritual path. This awakening of awareness on the inner, or etheric, plane of being is the safest and surest preparation for the activation of the head centres.

The *ajna* chakra, symbolized by the lotus with two petals, can only unfold when all the desires of the personal self are under complete control; when the emotions are so still and calm that the soul is like a quiet lake whose clear water reflects the surrounding countryside so exactly that it becomes like a mirror. The mind is trained and controlled so that it is still and waiting, the only thought being worship of the light, the quiet breathing in and out of the eternal Sun. In the stillness of this in-breathing and out-breathing the radiance of the spiritual Sun grows in intensity. The still water of the soul (*soma*—the Moon) becomes part of the great ocean of divine life, every drop of which is illumined. In this state of absolute stillness and illumination, the *lalata* chakra, situated at the top of the forehead, is activated and the soul can, at will, bring into the conscious mind any facet of knowledge which is required. This is cosmic consciousness, which we associate with Mercury, the messenger of the gods, manifesting his full power.

The Moon, mistress of the tides, has a natural affinity with Neptune, lord of the oceans. In ESOTERIC ASTROLOGY, Alan Leo suggests that when the soul has advanced to the stage where the head chakras are fully awakened, Neptune takes the place of the Moon and Uranus of the Sun in the horoscope. The emancipated soul realizes its Christed status as the Son–Daughter of the Father–Mother God.

Students of numerology will recognize the close affinity between the numbers 1 (the Sun) and 4 (Uranus); also between 2 (the Moon) and 7 (Neptune). Mercury's part in the attainment of cosmic consciousness, the blooming of *sahasrara*, the thousand-petalled lotus, links him with Pluto too, the planet whose influence brings awareness of the heights and depths of our being, and our close relationship with the endless galaxies seen and unseen in the heavens.

The control and stilling of the mind, and the direction of the thought by the divine will (which works through the heart-mind), is an essential part of the awakening of the head chakras. The consciousness rises on wings of light (the two petals of the lotus), and the crown chakra opens to receive divine illumination. The opening of this, the thousand-petalled lotus, brings a state of consciousness impossible to describe. The yogis call it *samadhi*. All who have touched it say that it is beyond description. It is a complete flowering of the three higher chakras—the heart, the throat and the head—which brings such a deep eternal peace, such an awareness of divine love, wisdom and harmony, that time ceases to exist. It seems completely inadequate to think of the astrological symbolism of the full Moon, except that the full Moon shining on the sea or lake on a summer night has a magical peace. It is truly an *awareness* of the celestial planes, which in our present state of development most of us can only touch occasionally; but once having seen the 'promised land', or touched that state of consciousness described in Revelation as 'the New Jerusalem', then like the children of Israel (children of the Sun) we cannot do other than 'keep on keeping on' (to use White Eagle's words), travelling towards it.

As followers of the White Eagle path we are blessed in that we have been given a way of service and devotion through the healing work and through our efforts to radiate the light to help humanity. Most White Eagle healers, especially those who work alone with the absent healing lists, work anonymously, with personal motives in abeyance, and no personal recognition, and yet they continue faithfully, without regard for feelings of adequacy or inadequacy. Yet this devoted service and steadfast aspiration towards the spiritual Sun is the finest, safest way to build the solar body; to strengthen and stimulate all the chakras, the psychic energy-centres, so that gradually every cell of the physical body becomes illumined with divine energy and light.

Ivan Cooke writes in THE TEMPLE ANGEL (now out of print):

'Human beings and angels are designed to work in conjunction and each needs the assistance of the other. The way to promote this bond and to develop a working companionship between the two is to remove angels permanently from their stained-glass-window environment and to come to look on them as co-workers. We shall surely find our angels when we are ready to become friendly with them, and might even see them more easily, when no longer blinded by earthiness. Surely we shall then grow in spirit, expand in sensitivity and power to see beyond the physical world. Angels are as much part of this world as are we, and people and angels ought to mingle here on this earth since both are responsible for its welfare.'

Every so often, when doing this work, the healer will be blessed with moments of complete happiness—moments of indescribable illumination, when the soul touches that centre of divine peace. The angels of healing, who draw close to help each individual worker, also help to raise the consciousness until, almost without realizing it, the soul becomes to some extent aware of heavenly realities. The healers who are able to take part in the special services for communion and rededication find that for a brief time they can rest from their labours and learn to open heart and mind to the blessing and illumination from the Great Healer. It is at these times of complete peace and self-dedication that we can perhaps begin to comprehend a little of the meaning of the illumination of consciousness which will come as the thousand-petalled lotus unfolds.

13

THE MAGICAL THIRTEENTH SIGN

THE THIRTEENTH sign of Arachne, linked to an actual constellation, that of Auriga, seems to function (as we have seen), not only as a sign in its own right, but as a little wheel driving the big wheel of the zodiac.

Its symbol, the equal-sided cross within the circle, has been used by secret inner brotherhoods throughout the ages. These are brotherhoods of souls drawn together by their search to find and follow the Pole Star, the pole star deep within their being, which links the individual to the heart of the Cosmos, to the heart of God—all-wise, all-powerful, all-loving. They seek the ray of light and power from that inner pole star which can transform the whole life.

Arachne, being of the subtle element ether, is associated with the Seventh Ray, that of ceremonial magic and the ray of the true psychic. Souls working on this ray often have in their birth-charts some planetary emphasis on the Arachne parts of the zodiac (that is, the last five degrees of Taurus and the first twenty-three of Gemini in the solar zodiac, or their polar opposite in Scorpio and Sagittarius).

The curious combination which Arachne demonstrates, through being the most subtle (Gemini), and the most practical (Taurus), of the zodiacal signs is a sign that magic must have a sound practical basis. We tend to think of it as a fairy-tale dream which has nothing to do with real life and is quite outside the scope of reason and common sense.

This is a false conception. Magic involves a thorough grasp of practical affairs and a command over them, together with a wise understanding of the foibles of human nature. It is a special branch of spiritual science, which involves calling upon the help of the angelic kingdom. The stories of fairies and elves helping the simple, kindly hero or heroine to find happiness and fortune are not just fanciful thinking, but part of the Ancient Wisdom. Yet help from the etheric kingdom of fairies, gnomes and angels always has a price. It involves obedience to the instructions given by the agent of this magic which brings power: power over material circumstances and, if used selfishly or negatively, power over other souls. There are angels of light and angels of darkness. The soul who would enlist angelic help is bound to keep to a bargain which involves either complete selflessness and devotion to the Christ light, or a selling of the soul to the angels of darkness.

The true white magician works entirely for love; love for God and love for all life, with no desire for fame, power or worldly success—only the will to serve God and humanity. Legends similar to that of Faust and Mephistopheles, in which the soul agrees to sell itself to the lord of darkness in return for worldly success and domination over others, can be found in many cultures. The path of magic concerns the subtle blend of the positive and negative aspect in every soul and a conscious invoking of the help of the angelic kingdom. Thought-power can be used or abused: the angels of light and darkness work together, and the tests on the path of spiritual unfoldment are constant and searching, for the safety of the aspirant. On the material plane, those who work with electricity or nuclear energy need strict training and obedience to the rules of safety. The cosmic energy which the soul begins to bring into operation through controlled thought-power demands even more training and wisdom. The only true power comes through union with the inmost spirit—that flame of the Christ Sun hidden within every human heart, a flame attuned to the heart of the Cosmos. From the innermost being there then shines a universal love which longs only to use the power of the spirit—the power which radiates from the heart of the Cosmos to heal and bless all life.

The student of magic learns early on that the death of the body is a mere incident which occurs many times on the soul's journey. The work, the study, the dedication continues. The soul will always return into incarnation along with its own brotherhood group, feeling an urge to follow the inner path of spiritual unfoldment, to serve with them on the inner planes of being; steadfastly working with them to find the deeper understanding of this divine healing magic which is the real work of the ancient brotherhoods of the Star.

The spider, symbol of Arachne, appears in stories and legends of many different lands. Often in these legends the little spinner of thread seems able to use a magical power to outwit its enemies or to steal from the gods a gift for the blessing of mankind. The web of the spider symbolizes the creation of a line of communication between earth and heaven. That silken thread is not unlike the etheric line of light connecting the soul and the physical body; the silver cord which allows the soul to travel on the inner planes during sleep or unconsciousness and firmly draws it back into the physical body on waking.

In many primitive cultures, spiders are thought to be lucky and helpful. In the western world, however, they are more often associated with magic and superstition—with witches and broomsticks and cobwebs in corners. A spider's web is not unlike a maze—the watchful spider lurks, waiting to devour unwary insects who become entangled and imprisoned, just as the Minotaur of Greek legend waited for adventurers lost in the labyrinth, and then attacked and devoured them. Such stories bring a warning to people who would dabble in super-physical phenomena or in practices which can force open the psychic centres, for a door can be opened to an etheric world fraught with mystery and danger as well as with beauty and enchantment. The silken thread of the cobweb is very like those psychic threads by which the soul can hold true and pure communion with the world of light; or, through lack of understanding and disobeying instructions, can become entangled in unpleasant elemental forces on the astral plane, enmeshed in a psychic cocoon from which escape is difficult.

While the solar zodiac fits neatly into twelve divisions, easily comprehensible to the intellect, thirteen is an awkward number, and one which has become associated with superstitions of bad luck and misfortune. Trying to explain this rationally, people often suggest that the fear of thirteen arises from the Last Supper and the betrayal of Jesus by Judas. More significantly though, it represents what is hard for the intellect to grasp: the non-rational, the mysterious. Throughout the ages orthodox establishments of mind and reason have tried to suppress the out-of-the-ordinary: for instance, groups following the inner mystical teachings. These teachings are common to all ancient religions and all great teachers; they are aimed at strengthening that line of light which reaches from the human heart to the greater self in the world of spirit, from which the 'little self' of every day can draw strength, protection and guidance.

The Moon is the queen of magic, and the number thirteen—linked with the lunar zodiac—has been associated with work on the inner planes and with matters kept secret and sacred. In the stories of King Arthur and his Round Table, there were twelve places for the knights and a thirteenth place, either in the circle or at the centre of the table, where sat the king. The table of King Arthur was actually the third of these tables of brotherhood, the first being the one at which Jesus sat with the twelve disciples, the table of the Last Supper. Here Jesus shared with his disciples the life-force of the Cosmic Christ, the spirit of the Sun, and instituted the communion sacrament of the Christian church. The second table, as well as the third, is located in Britain. Of these two tables, Geoffrey Hayward wrote in *Stella Polaris* (Vol.1, p.163):

'The second was the table of the Holy Graal, made in likeness of the first. From it Joseph of Arimathea fed 4,000 of his followers who came with him to Britain and were wandering in a forest; for he bade them sit down as at Communion, and taking only twelve loaves of bread set them upon the table before the Graal, and they so multiplied in its presence that all were fed. Afterwards Our Lord set Joseph's son, Josephes, in the position of master and pastor over the table, namely in the position where Jesus had sat in authority over the Twelve. This was called the Perilous Seat, which brought death or injury to any who falsely usurped it.

'Then came the third Table in the time of Arthur: "After this the Round Table was constructed, not without great significance, upon the advice of Merlin. By its name the Round Table is meant to signify the round world and the round canopy of the planets and elements in the firmament, where are to be seen the stars and many other things. Wherefore one may say that in the Round Table the world is accurately signified." And those coming from many lands, leaving all to become companions of the Round Table, were possessed by the gentleness and brotherhood of their fellowship; and through them, Merlin declared, the truth of the Holy Graal should be known. He therefore made a Perilous Seat at the Table, at which none but Galahad, then unknown, should sit, since he should be the leader of those who should fully achieve the quest of the

Holy Graal.'

Just as the thirteenth seat at the round table was the 'perilous seat' which could only be safely occupied by the pure knight who was wholly selfless, and seated there could share with his companions the life-giving healing of the Holy Grail, so also Arachne—the thirteenth sign—opens up a path of spiritual service which inevitably involves self-sacrifice and ultimately the crucifixion of the lower self.

This is probably why the number thirteen is superstitiously feared by those who are caught up completely in worldly interests, for while the thirteenth sign can open the gateway to heaven, it also demonstrates that heaven can only be won through sacrifice and self-giving. Souls who are beginning to respond to this line of light, the silver thread from the inner or higher world, feel a deep inner urge to serve all life. No matter what their worldly task, they perform to the best of their ability the work which their karma places before them, but their desire for service urges them to use their soul power in some way to heal, bless and uplift their companions. They accept that this dedication to an unworldly ideal may well bring them ridicule, suffering and even martyrdom. They are the healers, the carers, the musicians, the artists and the inspired leaders of thought who, with their vision focused beyond worldly matters, seem to have the power to raise the consciousness of those around them to a higher level where they, too, can touch eternal values.

Music indeed has a powerful effect upon our minds and emotions; it may set us dancing, or marching more bravely on a difficult stretch of road, or have the ability to lull a restless baby, or even raise our consciousness far above earthly problems and sadness by a beauty which seems out of this world. For this reason, musicians—both composers and artists—can play an important part in awakening the consciousness of humanity to new ideas, to spiritual inspiration and also to those changes of lifestyle which usher in a new era.

One such composer is Richard Wagner, truly a son of the magical Arachne, for he had both the Sun and Venus rising in this sign in opposition to Uranus, placed in Scorpio, the sign associated with the inner world and the after-death state. Jupiter and Mars, in exact opposition in the signs Leo and Aquarius (solar zodiac) or Cancer and Capricorn (lunar zodiac), also harmoniously aspect Venus and the Sun and release in Wagner an almost overwhelming energy and attunement to the angels of music—the music of the spheres. His nervous system was peculiarly adapted to be an instrument through which that glorious music would flow, for Mercury—the co-ruler of Arachne and also the planet of communication—is placed in the thirteenth house of his lunar chart and gives him a powerful inner drive to express the almost inexpressible harmonies which he was touching. Fortunately the helpful planetary aspects in his chart gave him splendid physical health, for his highly sensitive nervous system was often tested to the limit by the impact of the powerful angelic rays which flowed through him. The tremendous strain of the flood of psychic energy on his nervous system was at times shattering and can account for much of Wagner's apparently irresponsible and foolish behaviour in practical life.

It is recorded that when he was composing he was frequently overwhelmed by a great tide or torrent of sound and vision which enveloped him. When he first felt the impact of the Ride of the Valkyrie, he fell into a sort of faint or entranced condition. In his mind he had no idea how his music was going to develop, and sometimes the force and beauty which poured through almost terrified him. This is typical of a soul caught up by angelic powers, which are similar to the great natural forces of the elements.

The sensitivity and openness of his soul to divine

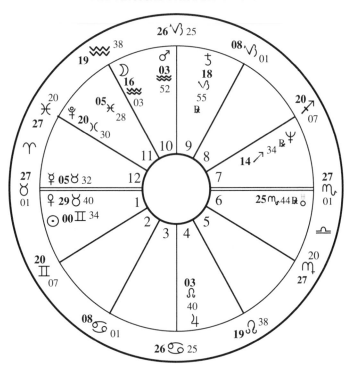

DIAGRAM XII: RICHARD WAGNER (SOLAR CHART)

MAY 22nd 1813, 3:07:00 AM GMT
LEIPZIG, GERMANY: 51N20:12E20
TOPOCENTRIC HOUSES

inspiration is shown not only by the Sun, Venus and
Ascendant in Arachne, closely opposing Uranus, but also
by the position of the Moon in Aquarius in sextile aspect
with Neptune in Sagittarius, the sign of the higher consciousness, of inspiration and prophecy, which is ruled by
Jupiter. Both Neptune and Uranus are in polarity with
Arachne (in opposite degrees of the solar zodiac). Neptune's position in the eighth house also links it with Mars,

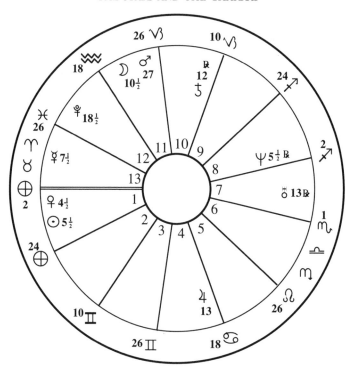

DIAGRAM XIII: RICHARD WAGNER (LUNAR CHART)

MAY 22nd 1813, 3:07:00 AM GMT
LEIPZIG, GERMANY: 51N20:12E20
TOPOCENTRIC HOUSES

the essential ruler of this house, and with Uranus in Scorpio (the eighth-house sign). As the Moon makes no other aspects, we see a personality highly sensitized by the beautiful neptunian rays which are subtly keyed to all the rest of the chart. These planetary positions all indicate a quickening of the throat and head chakras, which open his consciousness to the inspiration of the angels of music.

Comparing Wagner's solar and lunar charts, we find

that not only do the Ascendant, Sun and Venus now fall in Arachne, with Mars and Jupiter in their exaltation signs of Capricorn and Cancer, but that the house positions of the planets in the thirteen-house chart are even more clearly defined. Mars is now in the eleventh house of brotherhood and group work, but Saturn, which in the solar chart is seven degrees away from the tenth-house cusp, in the lunar chart is well inside it. This Saturn influence accounts for his conscientious hard work and utter devotion to his art. Neptune, which in the solar chart is just approaching the cusp of the eighth house, in the lunar chart is well inside it, thus emphasizing its magical position which clearly opened his soul to the inner world and to the reality of spirit. Also, Mercury in the thirteenth house instead of the twelfth now symbolizes an impelling inner urge to express in words and music the beauty of the angelic rays which at times possessed his soul.

Wagner always felt that it was from the people, the 'folk', that he must draw his strength and inspiration (Moon in Aquarius, solar chart); and that he was writing for the 'folk', who would intuitively accept these new ideas. In a sense this was true; yet the strength of the Sun and Venus in opposition to Uranus also caused him to be strongly authoritarian. He himself constantly rebelled against authority and the political establishment of his day, even to being forced to flee to escape imprisonment; yet in his own sphere he was a true leader, brooking no insubordination among his followers. It was said that when conducting he seemed to exert an almost magical power over singers and orchestra. His biographer, Ernest Newman, writes: 'Wagner had the born conductor's power to grasp the composer's intention and force it upon others. Above all, he possessed the dash and aplomb that gives confidence to players and singers who are none too intelligent or too industrious, and hides from the dazzled audience the thinness of the ice over which the performance had been skating.'.

Another friend writes of him, in a letter: 'When he conducts, he is almost beside himself with excitement...the orchestra catches his frenzy, and each man plays under a sudden inspiration.... Every sinew in his body speaks.... His whole appearance is of arrogance and despotism personified.'.

Only his family and closest friends knew what this cost him in nervous exhaustion. He himself writes: 'To be sure, people are astounded by the magic I appear to practise on the musicians; but no-one understands what the practice of this magic costs me.'.

There is no doubt that Wagner, through his music, was working on the Seventh Ray of magic. He was living at a time when a great effort was being made by the Brotherhood of Light in the higher spheres to break through the materialism of the dying age of Pisces and to reawaken humanity to the reality of spirit. This was the age when the Fox sisters were receiving the first tappings from the world of spirit, and when Theosophy and Christian Science were coming into being. Wagner himself was aware of all these new movements. He was a voracious reader and student, both of world legends and also of occult matters. One biography states that his wife, Cosima, was a medium through whom he obtained help and advice from the spirit world (Moon sextile Neptune, in the eighth house). He was a champion of anti-vivisection, and in his latter years became a strict vegetarian. He was devoted to animals, and on many of his travels and flights he was accompanied by quite a menagerie of pets. All these qualities of character are in keeping with the predominance in his chart of Arachne.

Music has an important influence on the soul life of humanity, and undoubtedly Wagner came with a mission to help awaken mankind from the grave of materialistic thought during the change from the Age of Pisces to that of Aquarius. The conflicts shown in his life and horoscope, and also in his music, are the conflicts of the whole human race, which is suffering and striving towards brotherhood, forgiveness and redemption. The theme of the storm-tossed soul transformed by divine love runs through nearly all Wagner's operas, as does the theme of the inevitability of karma. When the law is broken, retribution must follow. And yet the whole is ennobled and sweetened by heavenly love, the divine grace of the Holy Grail. Many of the themes of his operas, more especially his final work, *Parsifal*, were concerned with the inner brotherhood of the spirit, and the battle between the higher and the lower self through which the soul at last finds the Holy Grail.

14

ARACHNE IN ACTION

MANY FOLLOWERS of the mystical path may find themselves increasingly responsive to the thirteenth sign, Arachne, and also notice that their inner life is affected by the zodiacal positions and phases of the Moon. On the other hand, those whose karma causes them to be actively engaged in worldly affairs, which need a keen intellect and good reasoning power, will probably respond more to the rational solar or tropical zodiac. Neither zodiac is better or worse than the other. They serve different purposes in the soul life, according to the karma of that incarnation.

There is a very good analogy in the study of astrology itself. The reasoning grip of the outer mind (Sun exalted in Aries) is needed for learning the technique of setting up a birth-chart and the preliminary analysis of the planetary positions. When it comes to the deeper interpretation of these planetary symbols, the astrologer will find it helpful to withdraw from the outer mental plane into the inner silence of the soul world, the lunar world, in order to become receptive to the guidance from the plane of spirit. Guidance may be likened to the silken thread, the line of light to guide him through the maze of purely intellectual understanding.*

*The lunar zodiac chart can easily be calculated from the ordinary solar horoscope. Tables for the conversion are given in James Vogh's book; they are also provided in the Advanced Course of the The White Eagle School of Astrology.

A horoscope which is particularly interesting in the relationship between the solar and lunar zodiacs is that of Sir Arthur Conan Doyle, born 22nd May 1859 in Edinburgh. (Birth-times in Scotland are by law recorded, so the charts are accurate.) There is a considerable difference between the solar and lunar charts as the thirteenth sign Arachne, and the thirteenth house, are brought into such prominence. (Planetary *aspects* always remain the same.) The solar chart shows clearly the outer life of this great man, both his character and achievements, but the lunar chart helps us to understand more clearly his experiences after death, how he was apparently caught up in a psychic or etheric web, and also the mission he had undertaken on the other side. This we shall describe.

Because of the inner knowledge we have received from White Eagle about Arthur Conan Doyle's special mission, we can make a particularly detailed study of how he responded to his lunar horoscope and thus learn more about the workings of spirit and how Arachne spins her web. After Conan Doyle's passing, when his message (since reprinted in THE RETURN OF ARTHUR CONAN DOYLE, edited by Ivan Cooke) began to be received, White Eagle commented:

'This is a greater soul than even those who know him best have realized, and *has yet a noble mission to perform* [my italics]. Indeed his mission is more vital than anything he has yet accomplished. He calls to you, who are already dear to him, to help him in his service.

'He still loves the cause of Spiritualism. His whole desire was ever to give comfort to hearts which were aching and broken by the stress of life. That is why he crossed and re-crossed the world to bring hope and consolation to the bereaved and sorrowful. Now that he is released from his fleshly bondage—yet still limited by certain astral ties—his one desire is to press forward.'

In Arthur Conan Doyle's lunar chart, we see that instead of Gemini, Arachne, with its sign $\oplus$, rises and in this sign are placed Mars, Uranus and the Sun. Jupiter, still in Gemini, conjoins Mars and the two planets, as before, straddle the Ascendant, but all the planets which in the solar chart were in the twelfth house are now in the thirteenth, which James Vogh calls 'the house of the Inner Controller'—the house which shows the essential mission of the soul.

A typical son of Arachne, all through his life A.C.D. (as we shall call him) felt the urge to heal and help others, especially the 'man in the street' with whom he so often identified himself. From the events described therein, and the teaching which followed, it seems that like many araneans (i.e. subjects of Arachne) this soul knew before coming into incarnation that he had a mission—a great service to perform. In essence it was to demonstrate to the ordinary people, so dear to his heart, that a line of light—indeed a bridge of light—could be established between heaven and earth that would remove what White Eagle called 'the mad fear of death'. He also had to help people to understand the tremendous power of thought on the life, both here and hereafter.

Sir Arthur trained as a doctor at Edinburgh University but after a few years of medical practice he discovered that his stories, written in odd moments between patients' visits, were far more lucrative than medicine, so in May 1891 he decided to leave his practice and take up writing as a profession. He described this decision as 'one of the great moments of exultation of my life'.

That he was a born story-teller is very clearly shown in his solar horoscope which has four planets, the Sun, Uranus, Mars and Jupiter, all rising in Gemini, the mercurial sign of communication. Mars and Jupiter, fiery planets of energy and aspiration, rise on either side of the

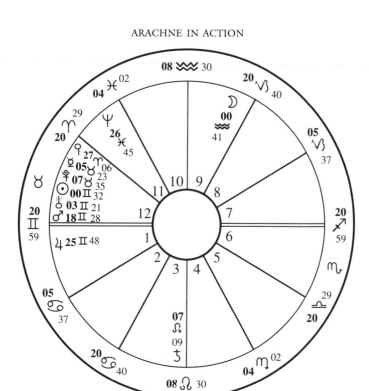

DIAGRAM XIV: SIR ARTHUR CONAN DOYLE
(SOLAR CHART)

MAY 22nd 1859, 4:59:27 AM GMT
EDINBURGH, SCOTLAND: 55N57 : 3W13
TOPOCENTRIC HOUSES

ascending degree, twenty-one of Gemini, which indicates
his tremendous vitality, and the sheer joy of life which
manifests in his writing. (Note the conjunction of Uranus
and the Sun close to the Ascendant, which can awaken the
joyous command of the *ajna* chakra.) Mars and Jupiter
together indicate his love of sport, his immediate readiness

170

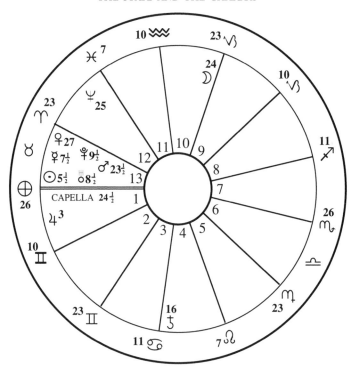

DIAGRAM XV: SIR ARTHUR CONAN DOYLE
(LUNAR CHART)

MAY 22nd 1859, 4:59:27 AM GMT
EDINBURGH, SCOTLAND: 55N57 : 3W13
TOPOCENTRIC HOUSES

to stand up for the under-dog and support 'lost' causes, and his zest for any kind of adventure. Writing was never any effort to him. As a schoolboy he could keep his classmates enthralled with his stories and just at an exciting point would stop and demand some kind of payment in the form of sweets, or trifles of value to schoolboys, before he would continue and relieve the listeners of their suspense.

With the Moon close to the Midheaven in the sign of Aquarius (solar chart), Sir Arthur had a sure finger on the public pulse. Instinctively he knew what the public wanted; in fact he often used to refer to himself as the typical 'man in the street'. As a true son of Aquarius he liked to share the common lot. He understood the needs of 'ordinary people' and in his writing catered for these so well that he became one of the most highly-paid authors of his time. The Moon close to the Midheaven usually indicates one who is brought into contact with a wide public, and when, as in this case, she is well-aspected with the Sun and Uranus (and also Neptune), she brings great popularity. The Moon forms an exact harmonious aspect with his Sun, which conjoins Uranus in Gemini (solar chart; Arachne in the lunar). A strong Uranus always brings an element of the unusual into a life, and A.C.D. had exceptionally wide interests and many original ideas, all of which he followed with utmost enthusiasm. In every way he was a big man, generous in mind and spirit and a great humanitarian, putting his heart into everything he undertook.

During his latter years he willingly sacrificed his money, his fame and finally his life to forward the intellectually unpopular cause of Spiritualism. For many years he had been sceptical of psychic phenomena, until after the death of a close friend he received such evidence as completely convinced him of the truth of the afterlife. During the 1914–18 war he realized how desperately people needed the comfort of sure proof of life after death to help them through that terrible period of bereavement and loss. His espousal of this cause against the general tide is indicated by the square aspect of Mars and Jupiter close to his Ascendant with Neptune in Pisces, the mystical twelfth-house sign. Mars is the planet of the fighter and pioneer; Jupiter is concerned with religion, and Neptune with psychic matters; and both rule long sea voyages. This combination is therefore typical of his pioneering work in trying to prove to humanity the truth of survival after death. He travelled the world lecturing and doing constant propaganda work for the Spiritualist movement, the continual strain resulting in the heart disease from which he died. This form of death is clearly shown in his solar chart by the opposition of Saturn, ruler of the eighth house of death, to the Moon in Aquarius—Saturn being in Leo, the sign of the heart, and on the cusp of the fourth house which rules the end of life. In the lunar chart, Sagittarius governs the eighth house, whose essential ruler, Jupiter, is therefore concerned with death and the afterlife. It is significant that this planet is close to the Ascendant and conjunct Mars in Arachne.

We are told in THE RETURN OF ARTHUR CONAN DOYLE that after his passing this great soul did not seem able to manifest as he had believed he should. He discovered that communication between this world and the next was not nearly the simple matter he had anticipated. Although he managed to give to his family satisfactory evidence through various Spiritualist mediums including Grace Cooke, by means of convincing personal messages, with mannerisms and habitual expressions which came through in such a way that his children said, 'That's Pop alright', Mrs Cooke was not herself satisfied. She felt that despite their detailed precision as regards family matters, the messages had not the drive and force which might be expected of a man like Conan Doyle. She knew that she was not contacting adequately his true spirit.

We then read of the coming of the messenger from Paris, from the Fraternité des Polaires, who had received instructions from their master through what they called 'L'Oracle de Force Astrale' to get in touch with a Grace Cooke. The message apparently read: 'Arthur Conan

Doyle has appeared to us (to the Sages), and among the many interesting things of which he spoke was his decision to interest himself in and help the Polaire Group. Before his death he had promised his friends to give proofs and manifestations of the after life.... He will hold to his promise. But not yet: for the spirit of Sir Arthur still waits in his beautiful Scotland for the time of the meeting of the *red* and *violet* rays. This meeting alone will enable him to speak to his friends.'. The reference to the coloured rays is initially puzzling, but we shall see shortly that it had precise astrological connotation unrecognized at the time. We also learn in the book, through the oracle of the 'Force Astrale' that the soul of A.C.D. differed from most souls in that it had incarnated under certain earth rays of great power and significance. No common destiny lay before such a soul once it was able to assert itself.

Here surely we see the unusual power of Arachne, that sign which links heaven and earth, and which also links souls all over the earth in brotherhood with each other, with the 'goodly company in the world of light', and also with the angelic kingdom. The planets rising therein give extraordinary vitality to body and mind and indicate that the psychic centres were all quickened. In early life A.C.D. was not drawn to psychic phenomena—although he always had a natural interest in the occult (Mercury, his ruler, conjunct Pluto in the twelfth solar house and in the thirteenth lunar one). The healthy activity of the lower chakras released energies which gave him his tremendous zest for life. Ruler in the earth sign Taurus (solar zodiac) and Moon in Capricorn (lunar zodiac) gave him a good foundation of earthly common sense, together with saturnian foresight, determination and feeling of responsibility. The root chakra (Saturn and the earth element) was harmoniously active, and he felt a deep desire to serve humanity. Arachne often intensifies the desire to give one's life in service. That Jupiter and Mars were so powerfully close to the Ascendant shows that the energies of the sacral chakra and the solar plexus are also freely flowing, giving unusual strength on the astral and lower mental plane—that plane of desire which, manifesting through the Arachne Ascendant gave him such an irresistible urge to get across his message of truth—to convey to others the light which had come to him. By the end of his earthly life he had willingly sacrificed the desires that had hitherto held him in his longing to bring comfort and help to his fellows. When, after death, he realized that in some ways he had been mistaken in his understanding about the afterlife, the desire to put things right became even more urgent. Yet because of this unusual strength and stimulation of the lower psychic centres, and to prepare him for his mission to bring to mankind a clearer knowledge of the inner worlds, he was as it were caught in an etheric web after death and imprisoned on the astral plane. After he had seen the lightning flash of truth—that flash of cosmic consciousness indicated by Uranus conjunct his Sun, which illumined and transformed his understanding, the realization of his imprisonment led him to seek help from the ancient Brotherhood of the Star in the higher worlds.

Arachne, being a blend of Taurus and Gemini, has a natural affinity with the planets Venus and Mercury, and thus with the higher chakras in the head, throat and heart associated with them; but there is also a powerful affinity with the fixed star Capella, which is one of the stars of Auriga, the charioteer (see chapter five). The link with Capella, through Arachne, can expand the soul's consciousness beyond the limitations of the solar universe, to become attuned to the whole of the starry heavens, the Cosmos—for the human soul is truly related to that little wheel, which helps to turn the great wheel of the Cosmos. This is partly beyond our present human conception, yet nothing is impossible to the awakened soul attuned to the heart of God—at one with the centre, the dot within the circle.

It is significant that Capella was rising in close conjunction with Mars and the ascending degree at the time of A.C.D.'s birth, while in his lunar chart Mercury and Venus, the planets of Arachne, were close to the cusp of the thirteenth house (the house of the inner controller), Venus being in the martian sign Aries and Mercury in the venusian sign Taurus. As described in chapters eleven and twelve, these two planets can lift the consciousness above the earth into the higher mental and celestial spheres, so that after his release his soul was prepared for a tremendous voyage of discovery, reaching from the lowest to the highest spheres of consciousness. Note that Jupiter, the planet of travel and exploration, placed so close to his Ascendant, makes a powerful square aspect with Neptune, which in the lunar chart moves from the eleventh to the twelfth house—the house of imprisonment, and of the inner worlds.

For his journey on the great ocean of astral life and consciousness, A.C.D., like all explorers, needed the guidance of the Pole Star, and so was drawn to seek the help of the Polaire Brotherhood, a group which on earth had been formed under the guidance of Sages in the East only a few years previously; part of the ancient Brotherhood of the Christ Star which is destined to lead humanity into the new Age of Aquarius.

The gripping power of those threads which had remained unbroken at his death made it psychically necessary to hold a special meeting on 22nd May, the day of his birth, preferably at his birthplace, Edinburgh. By this means, at the time of the conjunction of the red and violet rays, and with the help of the Polaire Star Brotherhood, the soul of A.C.D. could be set free from its limitations.

176

How are these colour rays shown in A.C.D.'s horoscope? The two most important points in any chart are the Ascendant and Midheaven. A planet close to either of these will dominate and colour the whole life. Here we have Mars, traditionally associated with the colour red, rising close to the Ascendant, its fiery power augmented by the conjunction with Jupiter, the greater benefic. The Moon, queen of the etheric and soul world, mistress of magic and long associated with the colour violet, is elevated close to the Midheaven, and in exact harmonious aspect with the Sun, which signifies the human spirit. But the Sun, closely conjoined with Uranus (planet of the lightning flash of truth) is placed in the twelfth house in the solar chart, known traditionally as the house of imprisonment and self—undoing, and in the thirteenth in the lunar chart (the inner controller—the life's mission).

In the lunar chart A.C.D. has not only the Sun and Uranus in his thirteenth house, but also Mercury, Venus and Pluto. Mercury, as ruler of his Gemini/Arachne Ascendant, is specially important, and the conjunction of this planet with Pluto probably explains his facility in writing stories about things hidden and unexplained: detective novels, stories about things wonderful and extraordinary, unsolved mysteries. Pluto, planet of the underworld, signifies the heights and depths of human experience.

In his journey through the inner worlds after his passing, one of the points which was brought home to A.C.D. so clearly was the tremendous power of thought. He discovered that when a soul leaves the physical body it finds itself in a world of its own thoughts. He was brought face-to-face with the thought-creations of his own books and his soul was filled with anguish when he saw how ones of a more horrible nature persisted and continued to affect the minds of those who read his words. It was brought home to him what a heavy responsibility lies with a writer with regard to what his writings create in the thought-world, and he was filled with a burning desire to help mankind to understand the power of thought and to use it for good, for healing.

Astrologically, the world of thought, the mental world, is represented by the air signs, especially Gemini whose ruler Mercury is the planet of the thinker. The airy Aquarius is, of course, the sidereal sign of the coming age during which man will begin to understand, and use much more fully, the power of thought. It is therefore particularly interesting that in the solar chart A.C.D. has his Moon, planet of the personality, at the very beginning of Aquarius, showing that the message he was destined to bring through was for everyone in the coming Aquarian Age. It was destined to teach people how to use the power of thought, how to open their hearts to the light of the eternal spirit, and in that light to find true.communion with those they loved who had passed from the physical life—something quite different from conventional communication, which A.C.D. found often to be with astral shells or astral memories, even though it is normally considered to be psychic proof of the afterlife.

His lunar horoscope, then, clearly displays the entanglement of a great soul in the meshes of the astral planes beyond death, and a spirit burning to be free to give to the world proof, together with a wonderful vision, of the panorama of life here and hereafter, which it so sorely needed. Obviously the Wise Ones had chosen Sir Arthur for this work long before his birth and were watching over his progress. His active earthly life, with his wide experience and skill as a writer, could be put to their full use in this unusual mission. But the Wise Ones knew that before Sir Arthur could speak with knowledge and authority he must be shown, and himself traverse, a wide range of the heavenly spheres. 'No one can escape his destiny, no matter how great, how strong, how good he be. Not even Christ could escape his cross.' (THE RETURN OF ARTHUR CONAN DOYLE).

In A.C.D. we have a gallant and noble soul, a trained and experienced writer and a pioneer filled with the desire to find and teach spiritual truth. His great love of humanity and an inner sense of his destiny irresistibly drew him to the work of Spiritualism which many of his friends in the literary world considered to be his undoing (Sun in the solar twelfth house, the house of self-undoing, but the lunar thirteenth house of the inner controller).

His progressed horoscope at the time of his passing is extremely interesting. Astrologers find this by counting forward a day for every year after birth. A.C.D. died soon after his seventy-first birthday, so we set up the chart for his birth-time seventy-one days later. We also count backwards seventy-one days from the birth-date to find the planets' converse position. Both these charts show significant links with the future work. In his natal chart, by converse direction the Midheaven opposes Uranus, the light-bringer; while converse Uranus was exactly on his natal Sun and converse Moon was coming to the conjunction of his natal Mars (the red ray which bound him to the earth).

The planetary positions in the solar chart on 22nd May 1931—the anniversary of A.C.D.'s birthday—the day set by the Sages for his release, show that the Moon, planet of the violet ray, had just passed into Leo, in which sign Mars, planet of the red ray, was also placed. In the lunar chart both were in the Moon's own sign of Cancer, further emphasizing the violet ray. At the time set for the group— 6.00 pm—Mars had just passed over the Midheaven and the Moon was approaching it, so it is likely that at the time of the release of this soul the Midheaven was exactly at the mid-point of these two planets. This could certainly be defined as 'the meeting of the red and the violet rays'. It is perhaps also significant that Mars and the Moon were both in Leo, ruled by the Sun (solar chart) or in Cancer, ruled by the Moon (lunar chart); interesting also, that his native Scotland comes under Cancer. On this 'two-two day', A.C.D.'s birthday, the Sun was of course in Arachne and in the same position as at his birth.

The interesting point about the group of souls drawn together in this work is the extraordinary degree of harmony shown between the one in the world of light and the one on earth which was enabled to help A.C.D. to fulfil his mission. It is surely no coincidence that he had such a powerful satellitium of planets rising in Gemini/Arachne, the sign of communication through speech and writing, while Grace Cooke also had an important and powerful satellitium of planets in Gemini/Arachne placed in the eighth house, which rules the after-death state, with Scorpio, the eighth-house sign, rising. What could better indicate the building of a bridge of light between these two, clear and strong enough to convey, to those still on earth, teaching from the higher worlds far beyond the plane of astralities. Surely, too, it is significant that his ruler, Mercury, was not only in Taurus—sign of the builder and of the heavenly temple—but also in the thirteenth house, the house of the soul's mission, the inner controller.

After the teachings came through, Ivan Cooke spent many months arranging and editing them for the book which was first published under the title THY KINGDOM COME, and many years in editing the White Eagle magazine which further amplified these teachings. Born on 22nd May, the same day as A.C.D. (as also Richard Wagner!), Ivan Cooke too had a powerful satellitium of four planets (including his Sun) in Arachne, close to those in A.C.D.'s chart, while his Mercury in Gemini was close to A.C.D.'s Jupiter.

There are many other links between these three charts and the time chosen for A.C.D.'s release, showing how these souls were drawn together by a power quite outside themselves, and by events over which they seemed to have little control—surely indicated by Arachne, the sign of the ancient brotherhoods, whose web of psychic links draws together souls from all over the world to continue their special work on the plane of thought, and which will become increasingly active in the New Age.

The charts of the two sisters (Grace Cooke's daughters, of whom I am one) who were asked to take part in some of the groups when A.C.D. was giving the teaching (to lend extra power) and who later found their lives completely dedicated to the furthering of A.C.D.'s mission, have similar planetary configurations in Arachne.

After the publication of THY KINGDOM COME (now THE RETURN OF ARTHUR CONAN DOYLE), it was hoped that all A.C.D.'s Spiritualist friends would welcome his fresh discoveries about life after death and the extraordinary proofs of his return, but soon came the realization that it takes more than a book to change people's minds and lives. White Eagle then gave the message that a centre was to be formed, first in London and then, later on, in the country, which was to be a focal point from which the Star Brotherhood in the world of spirit could work with those on earth, to radiate light and healing all over the world; a centre which would become as a lighthouse, to guide storm-swept souls safely into harbour, and help humanity through 'the years of fire' which lay ahead.

So after much planning and preparation the White Eagle Lodge was brought into being, and dedicated by White Eagle on 22nd February 1936. Soon a steady stream of books and pamphlets was being published and distributed, with the sole purpose of bringing comfort and enlightenment to souls in need, especially during the dark days of World War II. The original messages from A.C.D. were the basis of this work.

It is interesting to compare his birth-chart with that of the original White Eagle Lodge in London and to notice that his Venus (the planet of the heart chakra) is close to the Lodge Midheaven. His Moon conjoins Venus in the Lodge chart, surely indicating his warm interest in the work, while his Ascendant is exactly opposite Jupiter in the Lodge chart, and the Lodge Ascendant conjunct his progressed Saturn at the time of his passing. Saturn is the planet of long-term plans and of things which are intended to stand the test of time.

The links between A.C.D.'s chart and that of the Temple (opened many years later, in 1974) seem equally significant. The Sun in the Temple chart (which is the same as Grace Cooke's as it was dedicated on her birthday) is conjunct A.C.D.'s Mars and close to his Ascendant, while the Moon in Aquarius is almost conjunct A.C.D.'s Midheaven. The Midheaven of the Temple chart is close to the progressed Venus of the time of his passing.

Immediately after A.C.D.'s death much talk and argument arose about his memorial, for which a sum of only £2,000 was collected. There was so much disagreement about how this should be spent that eventually the money had to be returned to its donors. On 30th October 1930 White Eagle, as spokesman of the Sages, said: 'The underlying principle on which the work of the Memorial must rest is that this brother's [A.C.D.'s] name must be employed, not for the furtherance of his personality but, as his life was spent, for the establishment of truth and justice. *In this manner his name will be used after the death of his body to bring to the Brothers the power they need to build on earth a temple of the spirit.*' [my italics].

It surely seems a gracious and beautiful outworking of karma that this soul, who after death was so filled with remorse when he saw the effect of his writings on the minds of so many people, should be enabled to throw his tremendous energy and enthusiasm into sending forth teaching which would turn men's minds towards the light, comfort them in times of sorrow and perplexity and help them 'to overcome the mad fear of death'. There can surely be little doubt that Brother Nobleheart (as White Eagle called A.C.D.) is still an active worker for the true spiritualization of mankind, leading them into the Aquarian Age, and that the White Temple on New Lands hill is the memorial prophesied in October 1930.

15

BROTHERHOOD WIDE AS THE WORLD

IN ALL THE horoscopes we have discussed, Arachne and the element ether are much emphasized, which is interesting not least for the fact that White Eagle has often spoken of the etheric bridge which is being built between the two worlds at this present time. The basis of that bridge is always love, pure love in the heart, which enables the soul to establish and become increasingly conscious of that line of light into the inner world which, with practice, aspiration and dedication, can broaden into a veritable highway along which the shining beings from the heaven world can come to give their strength and help. Even while we have to be about our practical earthly business, this line of light, like Ariadne's silken thread, will lead us through the labyrinth no matter what problems we face, and bring us safely home.

Many people have asked, now that Mrs Cooke, Minesta, has left her physical body, whether White Eagle still gives his guidance in the work. Does he use another medium? The answer is simple. White Eagle continues to speak to all who attune to his vibration or ray. He also speaks *through* the intuition of all who attune to his vibration or ray, although if that attunement is in any way disturbed by the outer mind or by the claims of the lower self, his message is similarly affected. His work, during Grace Cooke's lifetime, was devoted to building 'the bridge of light' between 'his' world and ours. It is precisely because this bridge is so strong that his inspiration can be reached by all who truly listen. White Eagle's own personality, though, the one we have to come to know so well, is deeply associated with his own medium. Only when Minesta's daughters are speaking, as she did, on the platform in services at the White Eagle Lodge, or others very closely associated with her are taking services, do we normally hear his familiar voice.

White Eagle himself is the channel for a greater being—the Master of the Star Brotherhood. So the line of light extends from earth to heaven, kept bright by the love, dedication and service of the souls involved. Grace Cooke devoted her life to the service of White Eagle and the Star Brotherhood in the world of light. Although she is in spirit, her heart is still in the work which she now views from a finer vantage point. The link with her is unbroken; she is still the mother of the White Eagle family. Between her and every soul who looks upon the Lodge as their spiritual home there is a shining thread of light and love, like the silken thread of Ariadne, a line of communication heart to heart, which immediately enables her, as it does White Eagle, to be aware of and respond to any call for help. She works very closely with her family through the deep love of the ages which has been built up between them.

There is nothing haphazard about the plan which brought the White Eagle Lodge into being; neither is there anything haphazard in the plan for strengthening and consolidating the bridge of light during the years ahead. We pray that from it will develop in many Lodges all over the world, centres where souls battered by life and confused in the wilderness of modern thought can go to find peace, healing and soul refreshment which will strengthen and help establish their own line of light into the inner world.

It is interesting that during 1952, long before we had any knowledge of the lunar zodiac and the thirteenth sign, White Eagle was speaking of how we are linked together by slender threads similar to the threads of a spider's web:

'This work was begun and established not by the will of man, but by the will of the spirit. Such a work cannot come to fruition in a day; it takes long in preparation. You may be surprised to learn that many of the workers and friends of this Lodge have been prepared for a long time as you count time, and even during past incarnations. When such work has to be done you come back again and as if by magic are drawn together from all parts of the earth. For you have been linked together by slender threads which we will liken to the threads of a spider's web. You are linked not only to souls incarnate, but also to the great company of the discarnate. You are all one brotherhood, linked together by gossamer threads of spirit.

'Brotherhood is primarily of the spirit. Brotherhood is a harmonizing of thought and work and ideals. This is the foundation of the building of our temple.

'Remember that the cornerstone of the building of a spiritual temple is the Christ spirit and the Christ love, without which the temple cannot stand. We would remind all friends and brothers of this truth. Let the spirit of Christ be built into your building and it will stand secure, and its work endure.

'This Lodge was brought into being not by the will of man, but by the will of God, and by the inspiration and guidance of the brethren behind the veil.

'Of this company of the ancient White Brothers, some are known to you, others are not. All are with you, helping in the work. So long as all concerned with this work keep themselves attuned to that Brotherhood behind the veil, they can be sure that the work will continue to be blessed and sustained. Whoever you are, if you are attuned to the

Brotherhood of the Christ light you will be used.'

Those ancient brothers who built their stone circles so accurately aligned to the heavens, have left for a future age a symbol of the glory of the heavens which can be awakened in every individual soul. The circle of stones, surrounding a central stone and aligned to a particular star, symbolizes the human heart attuned to the Star in the heavens, through which it becomes illumined by divine power, wisdom and love. This awakens and energizes all the chakras, until every part of the being, physical, astral, mental and celestial, is radiating light and colour, sound and fragrance. Each of the chakras is alive with energy, sounding its own note in the harmony of the spheres. The soul is filled with divine life and power which then goes out to bless the whole world.

But from the moment that the soul awakens to the guiding light within, there comes a magical link with other souls all over the world who are drawn together by threads of light, rather like the spider's web—drawn into a brotherhood of the spirit, deeper and stronger than ordinary human friendships—united by a love of the ages which is untouched by the death of the physical body. Through many incarnations these souls, dedicated to the service of humanity, are drawn into a brotherhood whose individual light blends into a great Star of the Christ light, generating a healing power which can eventually raise the vision of the whole of humanity to love. This service continues and grows through many lives, and the spiritual power created in these small closely-united groups is like the little wheel which influences and drives the great wheel of human life and thought, just as Arachne—the magical thirteenth sign of the lunar zodiac—has been described as the little wheel driving the great wheel of the heavens. In the teaching of the ancient brotherhoods, 'Man, know thyself, and thou shalt know God and the Universe.'

Small brotherhoods all over the world even now meet for service on the inner or spiritual plane of being, some consciously co-operating with the angels of the Star to bring the Christ light to their fellows, and to all humanity, as did their more advanced brothers of the ancient stone circles. Through controlled thought and aspiration to the Star, the altar in each individual heart is quickened by it and begins to blaze with light and healing power which energizes and illumines all the chakras; reaching to the inner consciousness of other souls to awaken in them also a feeling of love for God and for each other.

The conquest of self, the overcoming of egotism, and the acceptance of divine discipline, has been the aim and the work of the brotherhoods in mystery schools throughout the ages. The ancient symbol of these brotherhoods, carved on rocks and stones the world over, is the equal-sided cross within the circle, the symbol of Arachne—or Ariadne, the most pure—or the Celtic lunar goddess Arianrhod who holds in her hands the silken reins which guide and control the inner life of mankind.

The special work and study of these inner brotherhoods was man himself, that each individual might be trained to develop and strengthen the godlike powers hidden deep within, and bring them into action in dedicated service. Through the unfoldment and development of the energy of the chakras, the soul gradually becomes able consciously to contact all the spheres of spiritual life and to use their powers as and when needed, even though still functioning in the physical body.

Always we find the theme: not of selfish personal ambition, either in earthly work or advancement on the spiritual path, but of dedication to the ideal—to the laying down of the 'little self' for the good of the whole. This attunes the soul—indeed the group-soul of the brotherhood—to the divine magic, the power which holds the stars and planets in their courses and orders all life according to perfect law.

BOOKS REFERRED TO IN THE TEXT

Jenny Beeken, *Yoga of the Heart*, Liss, Hants., White Eagle Publishing Trust, 1990

Grace Cooke, *Meditation*, Liss, Hants., White Eagle Publishing Trust, 1955

Ivan Cooke, ed. *Thy Kingdom Come*, London, Wright & Brown, 1933

Ivan Cooke, ed. *The Return of Arthur Conan Doyle*, 4th edition, Liss, Hants., White Eagle Publishing Trust, 1980

Joan Hodgson, *Wisdom in the Stars*, 3rd edition, Liss, Hants., White Eagle Publishing Trust, 1973

Joan Hodgson, *Astrology, the Sacred Science*, Liss, Hants., White Eagle Publishing Trust, 1978

Joan Hodgson, *Planetary Harmonies*, 2nd edition, Liss, Hants., White Eagle Publishing Trust, 1990

B. K. S. Iyengar, *Light on Yoga*, London, George Allen & Unwin, 1966

B. K. S. Iyengar, *Light on Pranayama*, London, George Allen & Unwin, 1981

Brother Lawrence, *The Practice of the Presence of God*, London, 1926

C. W. Leadbeater, *The Chakras*, Wheaton, Illinois, The Theosophical Publishing House, 1927

Alan Leo, *Esoteric Astrology: a study in human nature*, London, L. N. Fowler, 1967

Alan Leo, *The Art of Synthesis*, London, L. N. Fowler, 1968

Ernest Newman, *The Music of Richard Wagner*, Cambridge, Cambridge University Press, 1933

Apa Pant, *Surya Namaskars: an ancient Indian exercise* (by Bhawanrao Pant Pratinidhi, Rajah of Aundh, as explained to his son, Apa Pant), Bombay, Sangam Books, 1970

James Vogh, *Arachne Rising: the thirteenth sign*, London, Granada Publishing, 1977

White Eagle, *The Living Word of St John*, Liss, Hants., White Eagle Publishing Trust, 1979

White Eagle, *The Path of the Soul*, Liss, Hants., White Eagle Publishing Trust, 1979

White Eagle, *Spiritual Unfoldment 2*, Liss, Hants., White Eagle Publishing Trust, 1969

INDEX OF PRINCIPAL SUBJECTS

THE WHITE EAGLE PUBLISHING TRUST is part of the wider work of the White Eagle Lodge, a meeting place or fraternity in which people may find a place for growth and understanding, and a place in which the teachings of White Eagle find practical expression. Here men and women may come to learn the reason for their life on earth and how to serve and live in harmony with the whole brotherhood of life, visible and invisible, in health and happiness.

Readers wishing to know more of the work of the White Eagle Lodge may write to the General Secretary, The White Eagle Lodge, New Lands, Brewells Lane, Liss, Hampshire, England GU33 7HY (tel. 01730 893300) or can call at The White Eagle Lodge, 9 St Mary Abbots Place, Kensington, London W8 6LS (tel. 0171-603 7914). In the Americas please write to Church of the White Eagle Lodge, P. O. Box 930, Montgomery, Texas 77356 (tel. 409-597 5757), and in Australasia to The White Eagle Lodge (Australasia), Willomee, P. O. Box 225, Maleny, Queensland 4552 (tel. 0754 944397). A variety of activities is held at all these addresses.

All the White Eagle books are available by mail order from the above addresses but try your local bookstore first.